W9-ABI-352

Public Argument

Robert O. Weiss

University Press of America, Inc.
Lanham • New York

Copyright © 1995 by
University Press of America,® Inc.
4720 Boston Way
Lanham, Maryland 20706

3 Henrietta Street
London, WC2E 8LU England

Library of Congress Cataloging-in-Publication Data

Weiss, Robert O. (Robert Orr)
Public Argument / Robert O. Weiss
p.   cm.
Includes bibliographical references and index.
1. Debates and debating. 2. Public speaking. 3. Persuasion
(Rhetoric)   I. Title.
PN4181.W37   1995   808.53--dc20   95-3478 CIP

ISBN 0-8191-9900-1 (pbk: alk. paper)

Contents

Preface

The unique approach of this book is that it is consistently audience-centered. Its bottom line is that sound social decision making ultimately rests upon rational human judgment and the considered assent of the participants.

In the larger sense, *Public Argument* is devoted to the improvement of communication in the public sphere. When Júrgen Habermas defined the public sphere as "that realm of discourse in which something approaching public opinion may be formed," he pointed to a significant function for communication and argumentation.

Democracy depends upon meaningful public participation. Communication and argument facilitate deliberation about issues which call for general debate, consensus and decision.

Argumentation is reason-giving discourse. This book is intended to explore how members of a community may come to agree upon reasonable courses of action through talking with one another. Debate is a structured format designed to examine the reasons being given in support of contradictory positions on a given topic.

Now it happens that scholarly consideration of argumentation theory has taken a decidedly rhetorical turn in recent years, becoming especially conscious of warranted advocacy as public practice and of argumentation as "a function of the audience being addressed" (a phrase from Chaim Perelman). Practical reason and informal logic are getting methodical treatment. Meanings are contextual. General agreement and consensus among the citizenry are seen as normative goals. The whole rhetorical tradition seems rejuvenated, along with the view that argument should function as a meaningful social phenomenon. It is therefore in an intellectual environment of a revitalized argumentation that the audience-oriented perspective of this book on public argument is being offered.

The topics covered in the following chapters are on the whole traditional ones in argumentation, and the repositioning and redefinition of a number of concepts is designed to give the audience a central role while retaining the strengths of rational discourse.

Throughout *Public Argument* you will note that face-to-face audience debate is maintained as the model format for argumentation. However, it takes little imagination to extend the primary features of the audience debate to interpersonal or mediated formats. The public argument perspective can in practice be applied to a broad range of communication situations and contexts.

SCENARIOS

The concepts discussed in this book are being used in courses in argumentation and debate which operate with an audience perspective, where human judgment is respected, where genuine communication is important, and where audience assent is the guide to rationality. This material is also being used by debating societies and debate teams which are audience-centered in their perspective.

Although most of our specific examples are related to debating in an academic context and reflect an oral, face-to-face form of debate, the basic principles are equally usable by any civic organization which promotes intelligent discussion of public affairs, and they furthermore apply as well to electronically or print mediated-controversies.

Argumentation Courses. A University course in argumentation can be conducted with a public argument perspective, an approach which makes this book especially appropriate. As a matter of fact, these chapters have been used by more than 1000 students in such a course at my own university during the past 10 years. This particular course centers on a series of classroom debates set up in a parliamentary format in which substantial class participation is incorporated. Everyone in the class has the opportunity to speak in each debate. Furthermore, debates in other formats, speeches of advocacy, discussions, papers and exercises have augmented the exploration of audience-oriented principles of argument. Finally, supplemental lectures and reading resources are also incorporated in the syllabus. Chapters 3-12 are tailor-made for an argumentation course.

.**Forensics Programs.** The material in *Public Argument* is equally addressed to any co-curricular forensics program which focuses on genuine communication to real audiences. If you are involved in forensics as a director, coach, or participant, you will use competitive activities as practice for appearances before a variety of audiences. Opportunities for public presentation will be part of the schedule. For instance, publicly announced debates will be set up and opportunities to speak at meetings of other community organizations, as well as on radio and TV programs, will be sought out. Individual events participants as well as debate team members will be part of these endeavors. In tournament competition it is possible, using some care, to find meets explicitly subscribing to an audience-centered philosophy. The Cross-Examination Debate Association was founded upon such an impulse and, more recently, the National Educational Debate Association has explicitly mandated a public argument approach. Chapters 2 and 13, as well as the other chapters of *Public Argument*, are especially meant for forensics participants in colleges and universities.

Civic Groups. Chapters 2 and 13, it should be said, are also useful for any kind of organization which promotes debate about significant public issues. For instance, a campus debating society will need to be aware of the managerial efforts necessary to maintain a successful program. Its members will have a laboratory in which public debate and argument are practiced regularly. Outside of the academy civic organization and governmental agencies sponsor debates and hearings to contribute to public understanding and decision.

ACKNOWLEDGEMENTS

Many minds have played their parts in the development of this material. The aforementioned 1000 students who have enrolled in the Public Communication and Controversy course at DePauw

University have reacted to it critically and constructively as we have incorporated it into their learning experience. A number of full-fledged co-curricular programs have been audience-oriented. The finest instance I know of was a program directed at the University of Illinois by Kurt Ritter with the assistance of his excellent forensics associates, notably Charles DeLancey and Mae Jean Go. The Debate Society at my university has maintained a continuous existence due to the energies and talents of a series of conscientious leaders. In my forensics program I have been helped in my thinking about audience-oriented forensics by many students, including but not limited to Bill Wickens, Mark Small, Katy Bachman, Rodney Johnson, Peter DeBenedittis, Tim O'Donovan, Barbara McHugh, Matt Miller, Kim Smith, Geoff Klinger, Kent Ono, Joel Hand, Patrick Johansen, and Chanda Coblentz. On the intercollegiate scene, Jack Howe's vision for CEDA and the founding of NEDA by Gary Horn and Larry Underberg have been important. Further back, I must note the influence of my father, Nicholas J. Weiss, himself a debate coach, and of Carroll P. Lahman, my debate mentor.

Finally, highly valued support and inspiration, as well as meticulous proofreading, were ever available through the collaboration of Ann Lenore Weiss in this enterprise.

Robert O. Weiss
DePauw University

Chapter 1

A Rationale for Public Argument

You can picture yourself standing at the podium in front of a crowded auditorium, defending (or attacking) gun control legislation, with opposing speakers scrutinizing your every word, with listeners poised to ask questions, with dubious looks on the faces of some of those listeners and delighted applause breaking forth from others, not to mention a few really bored expressions. If you can picture that scene, you can get some of the feel of what it's like to engage in public argument.

The situation is not necessarily so formal, of course. You participate in public argument whenever you get into a serious conversation about issues which are important to yourself and others, when you write or read letters to the editor, take part in a committee or club meeting, get into a classroom discussion, or attend a public hearing. No matter which of these situations you're in, you are contributing in an important way to public decision making.

Debating with people about important and controversial issues is the heart of public argument. A Kiwanis Club wants to know the pros and cons of a "value-added" tax. A college or high school debating society tries to decide whether to go on record as supporting a political correctness code. The League of Women Voters sponsors a "candidates" debate. Wherever there are citizens trying to figure out what to do or what is best, public argument in its many forms should flourish.

In public argument, the audiences who make the decisions are central to the whole enterprise. Audience members decide what's right or wrong, true or false, desirable or undesirable.

As noted rhetorical scholar Chaim Perelman insisted, "It is in terms of an audience that an argumentation develops."

Therefore, almost anything you would want to know about public argument is answered by referring to the audience members who are taking part in it. If you want to know what constitutes evidence in public argumentation, you simply ask what it is that audience members know or are willing to accept. It isn't evidence until somebody accepts it. If you are puzzled about how the wording of a proposition should be interpreted, you find out by asking what it means to the people who are sitting before you. Even if you ask what kind of delivery you should use in speaking, you remind yourself that the best use of voice and action is whatever makes arguments comprehensible and effective for the collection of "judges" who constitute your audience.

THE PUBLIC SPHERE

The locale of public argument is essentially what we may refer to as the "public sphere." And just what is the public sphere? As conceived by Júrgen Habermas, the public sphere is "a realm of our social life in which something approaching public opinion can be formed." Habermas goes on to add, "A portion of the public sphere comes into being in every conversation in which private individuals assemble to form a public body." In other words, whenever topics of general interest are being considered by members of our society, we have the public sphere in operation.

The preservation and enhancement of the public sphere, with more debate and discussion of public affairs by everyone, have importance for four reasons.

(1) Some fundamental values and assumptions of a society are markedly a product of consensus. Whether or not we subscribe to the values of democracy or have public positions on corporal punishment

are products of agreement among citizens.

(2) Some matters are important to large numbers of persons, or are of critical interest to some of them, so that their participation in debate about their own condition is essential.

(3) Rationality is a matter of agreed-upon judgments. Whether any position is reasonable may be best determined by allowing full and free debate about it so that human judgment may operate at its optimum level.

(4) Since social participation has a legitimating function, the implementation of decisions rests upon the participation in the making of those decisions by those who are supposed to carry them out and those who are expected to abide by them.

Pressures to limit the extent and influence of public sphere debate come from many directions. Claims of expertise and science, for instance, insist that there are spheres of decision which are too technical for ordinary citizens to understand. For another thing, the "private" sphere, in which individual actions are nobody's business but one's own, has expanded to protect even corporate economic enterprises as private and not subject to public scrutiny. Furthermore, an administrative or bureaucratic sphere continues to expand, where decisions are made according to arcane standards and frequently the self-interest of the bureaucracy itself, unchecked by effective public control. And, finally, the perennial influence of armies, money, and "power" of other kinds continues to be a significant threat to the influence of public opinion.

DEFINITION OF PUBLIC ARGUMENT

But let's now try to define public argument more formally, just so we'll be able to distinguish what we are talking about from other kinds of discourse.

Public argument, first of all, of course, is intended to serve a decision-making process. In a culture like ours we assume that people make deliberate and considered choices about what they do and the values to which they subscribe. When alternative courses of action are available, we have to make choices. If a zoning ordinance is up for adoption in our community, it can either be adopted or not adopted, and it is up to us to decide. A decision has to be made. Even if we are debating about more abstract values, such as the desirability of free speech or free enterprise, an audience is expected to develop an explicit preference, which is itself a kind of decision.

Naturally we want our decisions to be good ones, so we are going to be as rational as we can in making them. Being rational means giving reasons, and public argument is a reason-giving activity. In making a rational decision, we look for sound reasons which will guide us toward accepting or rejecting propositions set forth for our approval or assent. The form of discourse (speaking and writing) which we use in this endeavor is argumentation, which basically consists of propositions supported by evidence and reasoning. If we are trying to decide whether or not television cameras should be allowed into courtroom trials, we don't flip a coin, and we don't take somebody's word for it. We will examine the relevant evidence and reasoning in order to choose what to us seems to be the best course of action.

As we have suggested, many proposals which come out in public life contradict one another. You can't both have and not have those cameras in the courtroom. This is where controversy comes in, and this is why some form of debate is the characteristic format for public argument. Debate is a method for comparing the reasons set forth by advocates of contradictory positions. There's a pro side and a con side, an affirmative and a negative. Controversy and debate stimulate the challenge and testing of evidence and reasoning which gives public argument its validity. In an organized clash of ideas, some emerge as better than others. Contradictions become apparent, weak evidence is challenged, and alternative lines of reasoning are brought to bear on the question. When you debate, you are not only setting forth the reasons which support your side, but you are also answering the other side. They are doing you the same favor. In this way the audience in public argument is the beneficiary of the most thorough possible examination of the ideas of both sides.

Public argument takes this rational decision-making process into the marketplace. The fourth characteristic of public argument is that there are many people sharing and comparing their ideas on topics which are important to them. The topics are matters of common concern and ordinarily represent issues where public assent or support is necessary if action is to be taken. Public argument demands broad participation, which is one reason why effective communication is such an important part of it. We may not have a public debate on a private matter such as whether or not to purchase a used Camaro, but we will have a public debate on a myriad of concerns ranging from fixing potholes in the street to the adoption of a new constitutional form of government.

By definition, then, public argument consists of reasoned communication which is directed toward real audiences under conditions of controversy to gain their assent on matters of general concern.

The definition allows us to look at the features of the public sphere as we enter it and later to discover the necessary skills of analysis, reasoning, evidence, refutation, and communication which are necessary in order to be able to participate in public argument.

SO HERE'S WHAT YOU'RE DOING

Then what is so special about audience-centered debate? What fundamental values does it embody? We're going to suggest that the underlying values we reinforce in the best public debating can be identified in five prime clusters: informed public opinion, logical argument, human communication, honest conviction, and democracy. Although the discussion of these value clusters will be pretty abstract, try to keep picturing yourself engaged in the actual event, standing up there talking to your eager listeners and alert opponents, as well as some bored sleepy-heads.

You're Influencing Genuine Public Opinion

The public debate in which we engage is alive in a real world. It contributes to the formation of public opinion. It has this genuine and important function: to provide information and to clarify issues for persons who are actively involved in the subjects you are talking about. This purpose is the challenge of debate, and this is what's fun about it, too.

These topics are not lifeless and remote. People really care about them and in some cases are vitally affected by whatever happens in connection with them. If you discover that they don't care one way or another about your topic, then don't debate it. Find something else.

Once you're up there talking, you can't avoid becoming a genuine part of the ongoing process of public opinion formation in any event. All talk is influential. Any utterance which is heard and understood at all will have some kind of effect upon its hearers, so when we debate in public what we say makes a difference. If we contend that capital punishment is a good thing, someone just may get electrocuted.

We don't want to overstate the amount of influence you may have in one debate, though. You aren't some kind of magician who can speak a few golden words and change the course of civilization. Communication is hard work. The persons you are speaking to also read newspapers and magazines, they talk to other people, they watch TV to find out what's going on, and they keep their eyes open. You aren't the only one trying to influence them, but still your contribution is not without its effect.

Since everything we say is influential, an audience debate cannot be an empty exercise, a piece of fluffy entertainment, nor can it be a simple exhibition of skill or cleverness. This is not to say that a debate can't be entertaining; in fact it usually will be. But we can never say that "this debate doesn't count." Even a practice debate will count, will affect our opinions and perceptions in some way. Always remember that somebody may believe you when you talk.

Furthermore, if it is true that what you say is bound to be influential to some degree, and that you are taking part in a genuine societal deliberation of problems and values, then you are responsible for what you say. A public statement is a public commitment. The audience comes to a debate to think about the issues, not to see some smart aleck perform. You say what you mean and mean what you say.

In the world of public opinion even the most unpopular ideas may deserve a hearing. Thus, there may be times when you would see it desirable to present a case to which you do not personally subscribe, but be aware that most listeners will assume that you are serious, and therefore you will need to consider some troublesome practical and ethical questions on such occasions.

The swirl of ideas and opinions, popular and unpopular, compelling and half-baked, constitutes the social context where public debate operates. Every debate is different; the situation changes each time we debate. The arguments of public figures, the march of events, the changing values of our audiences will all influence the arguments we choose to use and the reception they will get. If we are debating the efficacy of the War Powers Act, a newsworthy occurrence such as the Gulf War will immediately produce new facts and new public attitudes which will add whole new dimensions to the controversy.

You're Thinking Logically

Your ideal as an audience debater is to influence people through the logical proofs you employ. When you enter this world of disciplined thinking, you're not trying to talk louder or faster or prettier than the other person, but to demonstrate the logical strength of your position by the evidence you present. It's a contest in who can be the most reasonable.

Aristotle defined man as the "rational animal," and among our highest human ambitions, as we suggested earlier, is to make our important decisions on rational grounds. We want to base what we believe on carefully considered reasons and all the facts we can get.

The centrality of logical argument holds for audience debate as well as for any other kind. Argumentation is widely and profitably studied as the methodology for justifying claims. If we are claiming that the air traffic control system is overburdened, we try to find the most knowledgeable and unbiased scholars to provide us with their expert testimony on the subject. If we are saying that cheating is a problem on our campus, we want to find whatever facts and examples are available to indicate how widespread it actually is.

One of the recognized preconditions of rationality is objectivity. We try to be objective by examining all of the available facts and other evidence rather than depending on our personal biases and prejudices. Just scrutinize the facts. An objective argument means one which may be checked by direct observation. Chaim Perelman suggests that objective argument is that which is addressed to a "universal audience." We're not going that far, since audience debate is addressed to particular, living, breathing human beings, and a complete objectivity is probably not possible and may not even be desirable. Like a news reporter, we may know that being completely objective is not possible, but we still try to get the facts as clearly and impersonally as we can.

In being a logical thinker, you also approach arguments, including your own and those of your opponents, with a critical attitude. You continually question whether the evidence is true and the reasoning is valid. Debate inherently includes this kind of questioning and this critical attitude because the other side is always right there. A critical attitude will lead you to be more reasonable because it makes you use the best possible proofs, discarding the ones which are weak and illogical. Furthermore, inconsistencies become apparent in the course of a debate. You can't advocate a new government spending program and then claim that you will lower taxes.

If you have studied logic before, you will soon recognize that in this book we are merely scratching the surface of all of the available methods for making sure that your proofs are logical. You are aware of potential fallacies, tests of evidence, how to analyze propositions, and the multitude of other standard debate procedures.

If you haven't studied debate before, then you will want to look into the work of rhetoricians, communication theorists, and philosophers who have themselves debated about what constitutes logical argument. Furthermore, read some of the great debates, such as those over the adoption of the Federal Constitution or the Lincoln-Douglas debates, to get the flavor of argument in action. There are literally hundreds of books about debate, and part of learning to be a logical debater is to know what you're doing by investigating the theories and standards which have been developed by scholars through the centuries.

In the last analysis, of course, we're going to trust our listeners to know a good argument when they hear one. They are the rational animals. For their satisfaction as well as our own we will maintain logical objectivity and reliance on the facts as a standard for our performance in the debate situation. That's what the world of logical thought requires.

You Are Part of the World of Human Communication

For all of its strain toward objectivity, public debating seldom consists of disembodied talk addressed "to whom it may concern." You're talking with real people, and these people add as much to the meaning of the argument as you do. All of your listeners process your arguments in their own minds. (If you are the audience member in this scenario, then you contribute as much to the argument as the speaker does.)

In the world of human communication, listeners are not like blank sheets of paper waiting passively for someone to come and inscribe reasoning upon them. They do not have to ignore personal feelings. They do not have to leave their brains at home. They contribute what they already know as they mull over what you are saying, and they apply the standards of reasoning which have worked best for them. Human communication is an interactive world; it is not a one-way street.

One debater claimed in a debate with a documented source, "35,000 infants die of starvation in the United States every year." Listeners were justifiably skeptical about this fact, reasoning to the effect that, "If it were so, I would have heard about it." This statistic would have appeared prominently in the papers or on a TV special. It just did not seem likely.

Naturally, some very unlikely facts are actually true. In employing unlikely facts, the speaker needs to use quite a bit of reinforcement to overcome natural doubts about their acceptability.

What you are doing as you communicate is providing material, such as evidence and lines of reasoning, which listeners process in their individual ways to reach their own conclusions. You can never say "You have to believe this" to an audience, except as a line of argument of its own. They can always say, "I don't have to believe what you are saying."

One implication of the fact that every audience member processes the debate in his or her own mind is that there are, in effect, a whole lot of debates going on in the room. That's the way audience debate is. Sometimes you will be surprised at what happens when you speak (and when you listen). "I didn't say that" and "I didn't know you would take it that way" are expressions all too common as people try to communicate.

In most formats for public debate the audiences are not limited to chewing on arguments in the privacy of their own minds. They are invited to participate actively and out loud in the occasion. In this way they can ask questions and find out additional relevant facts which they want to know. Furthermore, they can test their own arguments by setting them forth in the form of speeches and seeing what response they get. Or they can test the arguments of others by raising apparent objections to them.

It may be hard for us to believe that an argument may be logical for one person and not for another, may be logical at one time and not at another, or in one place (Colorado) and not in another (Rhode Island), or in one field (religion) and not in another (law). Still, the test of the acceptability of any reasoning in the final analysis is the response of the individual listener, and this response is inherently affected by the ideas he or she brought along to the debate.

This fact is indeed one of the virtues of public debating. It is a method for comparing facts and reasoning utilizing all of the human experience in the room. The process is not a computer print-out or an empty calculation, but a human communication enterprise.

You're Dealing with Honest Conviction

A decision in a public debate is somebody's actual, honest opinion about which side is right. When a vote is taken at the end of such a debate, you aren't asking "Which team did the better job of debating?" or even "Which team had the better case in this debate?" You're asking, "What is your opinion with regard to the proposition right now?" The judges in an audience debate are individuals making up their own minds about where they stand.

If a debate is conducted on the pros and cons of the proposition, "Resolved, that a Constitutional amendment should be adopted requiring that the Federal Government maintain a balanced budget each year," there may be members of the audience who believe in the affirmative side at the beginning of the debate and still think the same way when it is over. They haven't swayed a bit. Others may support the negative and never change their opinions. That's all right. They can go ahead and vote their convictions.

In still other cases, listeners may start out undecided and eventually decide that one side or the other is right, and yet others may change their minds completely while hearing the debate. Whatever their real opinions are on the question at the end of the debate, that is the way they should vote.

As a member of the audience, no "judge" is required to decide merely on the basis of what has transpired in this debate. Just because somebody failed to answer a particular point does not mean that the audience member has to accept it. It may be a dumb point. Think of yourself as the judge (which more often than not you will be) and figure out how you make your real decisions.

Besides that, these judges don't have to be completely impartial. All human beings have opinions. As a general rule, of course, debate depends upon relatively open-minded attitudes and a willingness to listen to and evaluate carefully what is said. If you're going to have an opinion, naturally it should be based upon a conscientious evaluation of reasoning and evidence, which requires a good deal of openness. It is true that some speakers and listeners have commitments which limit their ability to make objective judgments. They may even be paid representatives of some organization. Still the best audiences recognize any biases they have and listen to the reasons which are presented during the debate, even though no one has to pretend that he or she is completely unbiased.

Nobody can be forced to vote, either. Because a person may genuinely be undecided about a proposition, an audience member who is attending a public debate may legitimately abstain and not vote at all. In a parliamentary situation, an abstention in effect serves as support of the prevailing side. In that case, a resolution either passes with a majority or it doesn't. Still, the premise in this and other audience debating is that the individual is voting (or not voting) the way he or she really believes.

Some listeners may have strongly held beliefs, while others are less sure about where they stand. Thus the votes cast following a public debate may represent quite a range of intensities, even when those votes are counted on a simple "ayes and nays" basis. Although there exist ways of computing the strengths of attitudes which people hold, and you may want to try some of these out, most audience votes consist of a simple count of the majority and minority totals. What should be recognized is that not all those votes may mean the same thing.

People also change their minds. Almost all human decisions are tentative ones, representing the idea that "Here is where I stand at this time." Any public debate is part of the larger universe of public opinion and discourse, and the vote does not stand isolated in time and space, so new events and even new debates may generate changed decisions as time goes on.

The world of honest convictions consists, then, of human opinions which are somewhat biased, relatively tentative, varying in intensity, and subject to change. Public argument addresses itself to these opinions.

You're Entering the World of Democratic Values

The kind of problems we usually debate about in public are issues which involve a lot of people whose opinions count for something. Therefore, the processes of public debate are deeply entwined with the values of democracy, where decisions are made in the light of what people think and where everyone's voice is heard in the decision-making. When the society as a whole is deciding whether its resources should be devoted to schools or to warplanes, or when a specific community is debating about repaving its streets, the uppermost factor is the opinion of the people concerned.

This implies that people are capable of participating in a democratic process. It has been said that we should neither overestimate the information which the average citizen has nor underestimate his or her intelligence. Audience debaters respect popular opinion as intelligently motivated and in the long run sensible.

What about experts, then? Obviously experts are an important resource and we need to know what they think. Still, a public debate does not mean listening to an expert tell us the answer or tell us what we must think. This expertise is to be put at the service of the general public opinion process. If the expert is competent and relatively unbiased, and other experts are not contradicting him or her, we may be able to give great credence to these arguments, but they remain merely arguments, subject to every test the audience can muster on its own. If there are subjects which people are generally too ignorant to debate about, then don't debate, but also do not let that area of discourse become too large. As far as we're concerned, we should be ready to debate just about anything.

> If there be any among us who would wish to dissolve this Union, or to change its republican form, let them stand undisturbed as monuments of the safety with which error of opinion may be tolerated, where reason is left free to combat it.
>
> ThomasJefferson, *First Inaugural Address*

Responsible public debate, whether you are a main speaker or an audience member, does require preparation, of course. All who speak gain their right to be taken seriously from the amount they have thought about the subject and how much they really know. A basic grasp of the central issues of every public question is available to the inquiring mind.

Being prepared, we might add, also means being able to communicate what you know effectively. You can't just sit on it. A society in which debate flourishes is one in which all citizens are trained and practiced in communication.

Furthermore, for debate to flourish, the citizens must value freedom of speech, one of the essential guarantees of the United States Constitution. No one should be prohibited from saying what he or she thinks or presenting arguments he or she thinks are relevant. Freedom of speech is as vital to public argument as it is to the functioning of any democratic society as a whole. There may be overwhelmingly compelling arguments to refute what you have to say, but there can be no coercion to stop you from saying it. This even implies that there should be no questions which we are not permitted to debate, no matter how one-sided they may seem to some. If someone wants to defend anarchy, then let the debate proceed (with such rules as can be made relevant in such a case).

An audience debate is not an esoteric and arcane manipulation of data by presumed experts; it is a sharing of ideas among all of those concerned with important issues. When you enter the world of democratic values you are letting everyone have a say about the arguments advanced and everyone have a voice in the decision because you respect them as individuals.

What About Winning?

Debate looks a lot like a game. Usually a debate is set up with opposing sides who are competing with one another, it has rules of procedure and fairness, certain kinds of strategies are available, and it normally ends up with a win-or-lose type of decision. In such a context, you're naturally going to try to beat the other side and do all you can to win, aren't you?

As a matter of fact, debate can be conducted as a kind of intellectual sport, like chess, in which nobody cares very much whether any minds are changed or influenced. Actually, it's kind of fun, and beating someone at it can be ego-satisfying. Debate is something you can learn to be good at, and if you're improving your argumentative skills in that context, go to it.

However, beating other people is not what we're going to be talking about in the chapters ahead. We will be focusing on the process of testing ideas in the crucible of public opinion. "Winning" will mean that in that particular instance you have reasoned in a manner which has gained popular assent. The ego-satisfaction of successfully defending your beliefs may indeed make you feel good about what you are doing, and even the elements of interpersonal rivalry which motivate you to be especially rational in the face of a particular rival will not have to be ignored. But the bottom line in audience debate is influencing other people through strong arguments. That's what we will be concerned about.

It would be a little soupy of us to say that in audience debate everyone wins. But we can say that it is more than just a game. In the last analysis, real human decisions are at stake.

And What About Truth?

As we have said from time to time, the "worlds" we have been describing may seem abstract and removed from real life, but we still want to keep picturing those concrete situations when we are standing up speaking to an audience or else we are members of that audience participating as much as the speaker in the effort to reach a reasonable decision. Whenever this happens:

> We influence public opinion
> We try to think logically
> We communicate with one another
> We express honest opinions
> We reinforce democracy

In all of this, then, do we eventually discover truth? Can truth be discovered through public debate? Certainly there are hazards on the road to such an ideal.

For one thing, if truth is defined in terms too severe, as a quality so absolute that it cannot be questioned at all, then debate is hardly relevant to it. We dispute about probabilities, we develop and qualify opinions, and we grant assent. Probabilities, opinions, and assent are not absolutely sure things. We just don't usually argue about facts which we can check with direct observation (e.g., bananas are yellow), values on which there is universal agreement (e.g., the self-evident propositions of the Declaration of Independence), or matters subject to formal demonstration (e.g., a mathematical proof). Even in a trial where we might be debating whether Elmer burgled the toy store, an incident which could have been observed but wasn't, we can only argue when we have mixed evidence leading to contrary conclusions.

In every matter that is worth debating, both sides have much to be said for them. Both are to some extent right. There is no final "truth" about whether we ought to have bottle laws requiring that all drink containers be returnable. There is only a judgmental preference based upon the facts of waste and enforcement and the values of convenience and environment.

Even if there were unquestioned truth which could be determined, public debate would probably retain more modest goals. The barriers which interfere with intelligent decision making are considerable in any case.

Insofar as the participants want to be silly or don't care about the debate, the assent will hardly be well-reasoned. Insofar as the advocates neglect to investigate the question or prepare for the controversy, the decision process is not well served.

You can think of plenty of other hazards which can crop up in the pursuit of rational decisions. There are nuts and cranks out there, and they sometimes show up at public debates. There are acoustical problems and other forms of static. Even the debate format leads some individuals to distort and withhold rather than argue openly. These and other human elements may interfere with truth-seeking, or even with ordinary decision-making.

The objective of public argumentation, then, may not be the determination of truth per se. The objective is to facilitate the making of choices which are based upon strong reasons, in the face of hazards and difficulties, with the recognition that these answers are only probable, not final, and that what we are aiming for is intelligent assent.

Chapter 2

The "Public" in Public Argument

If we are talking about public argumentation, we have to figure out who is in this "public" which serves as its audience.

In the first place, we know that the public is not just one big, homogeneous glob. Even a national public opinion poll result is a composite of a sampling of many degrees of concern, of knowledge, and of bias. The public to which members of Congress respond consists of individuals and groups who feel compelled to communicate with them.

There are indeed many publics. A large proportion of the population may have a concern and engagement with certain matters of overwhelming national or global significance. More frequently the various publics may be identified demographically. We are an audience for discourse about issues that affect our geographic locality, our occupation, our economic status, or our religion. They hit us where we live. Furthermore, we seek out individuals who share our worries about "single issues" such as nuclear waste disposal, abortion, handguns, or classical music. And "mini-publics" may develop to debate about relatively temporary or local concerns. These many publics overlap throughout society.

And the public conversation does not consist entirely of

citizens sitting politely in an auditorium quietly contemplating the issues. It's a jungle out there. Much public discourse is shrill and strident. Powerful economic and political interests are playing hard ball. The people who are doing most of the talking are frequently "spokespersons" for various causes, advertisers, and public relations specialists. The means of communication employed go well beyond structured writing and speaking to include street demonstrations, managed dramatic news events, picketing, and anonymous threats. Furthermore, there are "gatekeepers" (editors, publishers, news directors, etc.) who control access to important channels of communication. To transpose this wild variety of communication activity into enlightening debate is an important part of constructing a rational public.

Finally, many situations exist in our society where both sides are not represented and debate is hardly encouraged at all. Members of the elite have the power to make decisions for the rest of us and frequently do not appreciate the scrutiny of the public. Technicians make decisions on the basis of specialized knowledge and regard the rest of us as too ignorant to participate meaningfully. Fanatics sometimes talk a lot, but since they are right and everybody else is wrong, they don't have much use for genuine debate. And revolutionaries and criminals have their own methods for achieving their ends, frequently preferring to remain beyond public examination.

All in all, then, public debate may best be seen as an "impulse," an activity directed toward applying human reason to the swirl of events around us within the cacophony of communication that constitutes our society and our world.

FINDING AN AUDIENCE

So where do we find all of this public debate going on?

Suppose we want to join an audience and hear a debate? Suppose we have something to say and would like to test our reasoning in public? Suppose we would like to encourage or sponsor public debating? What do we do?

Remember that we said public debate is taking place whenever anyone is trying to influence the opinions of other persons with regard to significant matters, where contradictory positions are represented, and where the participants are willing to use reasoned discourse.

Not all public debate fits perfectly into a stereotyped model debate, with delegated affirmative and negative speakers, timekeepers, question periods, etc., but there are plenty of activities which come close enough to it to meet our general goal of rational public deliberation of problems.

If you watch for the announcements, certainly, you will find debates sponsored by a myriad of organizations, including colleges and universities, civic groups, churches, "Y"s, special interest societies, and formal community forums. Public minded service and fraternal groups, such as Rotary, Kiwanis, Exchange, and Business and Professional Women, have "programs" at their regular meetings (which can easily be set up as debates), and even if you are not a member of one of these you may offer to sponsor or participate in a debate program for them.

Increasingly prominent as a forum for general debate about specific proposals of public concern is the "hearing" conducted by a governmental agency. Many such hearings are mandated by law. Besides the frequent hearings scheduled by national and state legislatures, you will find the federal Department of Energy conducting environmental impact hearings on nuclear waste disposal, a state highway commission holding meetings on a proposal for a new exit ramp, or a school board having open meetings to debate whether a certain public high school should be closed down. Such meetings are almost always open for public attendance and participation.

Debates between political candidates at every level of government are also becoming increasingly popular. Following a precedent and a pattern set in the Nixon-Kennedy debates of 1960, candidates face one another under the auspices of the League of Women Voters or other nonpartisan organizations. Although such debates tend to lack a focus on specific propositions other than "Elect Jane Blow," they do give us opportunities to respond to arguments and reason-giving. They are called "debates," after all.

When political debates are carried over the mass media, they characteristically involve a good deal of intervention by journalists asking questions, but the direct participation by audience members is lessened. But otherwise these programs are frequently excellent settings for the clash of ideas. Leading the way is the MacNeil/Lehrer report on public television stations. The format of segments of this program allows representatives of conflicting positions to talk, answer questions, and to respond to one another. Other news programs, such as the ABC "Nightline," allow for similar exploration of timely issues. Relatively serious talk shows, such as the one presided over by Phil Donahue, may also bring out some creditable debating and allow for participation by studio audiences and call-in listeners.

Legislative assemblies ranging from the United States Congress to local city councils are the setting for much significant and influential public controversy. The *Congressional Record* can give you a very good feel for many of the methods and maneuvers characteristic of vigorous public debate. Most of us are not members of Congress, of course, but we are on committees of some sort, and the same kind of evidence, reasoning, and refutation addressed to decision-making listeners can be found in even the most routine committee work.

Public debating does not have to be oral, either. Watch the debates going on in the letters-to-the-editor column, on the "op-ed" pages of the newspapers, and in opinion magazines of all kinds. You can put it in writing. Adversary journalism is a recognized genre which promotes controversy directly. You can get in on journalistic debate yourself on almost any topic you are concerned about.

And don't neglect the ordinary "bull session." Though the give-and-take of arguments within casual groups of individuals at any time of day or night may lack the rules and even the decorum of more formal debate, you can still match your opinions and reasons against those who think differently and get a lot out of it. Democracy is ultimately a great conversation, and you can participate in that with anyone else who is willing.

The opportunities are there already. Now we'll look into some methods for promoting even more such opportunities.

DEBATING ON YOUR OWN TURF

We're assuming that many of those who are reading this are in a formal college or high school situation. You're on a debate team or in a class, or you are directing or teaching a bunch of students who are. We'll talk mostly in these terms. However, if you're engaged in adult education, extension work, public forum activity, or public service or church groups who find audience debating functional in meeting your goals, most of what we're saying here (and in the rest of the book) is relevant to your situation as well. Read on.

No matter who you are, you can go to political debates, attend hearings, engage in bull sessions, and take advantage of other public discussion we've already described. But you can also look for and create special opportunities within your own educational situation, and here we'll look at some of the ways to do that.

Argumentation and Speech Classes

Debating is a valuable activity in a speech or (obviously) in a debate class at any level of instruction. All you have to remember in transforming the class into a public debate forum is that your objective is the expression of honest opinions and that everyone is participating in a genuine decision-making process.

It is possible to incorporate a single "round" of debate in a speech course devoted to a multiple set of objectives, but you may also arrange the whole course to use debate all semester, taking up all kinds of relevant, controversial issues.

In this kind of class you can learn a great deal about communication and the debating process while you are considering challenging public problems as you go along. You can experience many of the different formats which are described in the next chapter. Such a class has several key features. (1) You learn to do research, to use evidence, to reason, and to refute. In other words, you learn to think on your feet. (2) The assignments will be set up so that all of the members of the class will have opportunities to speak. In fact, they will no doubt be required to do so, and that will be good for them. (3) Finally, incorporated into the formal class structure will be critiques by the instructor and by fellow students designed to improve individual performance and the quality of the group's debating as a whole.

This is one audience that is dependable in that it can be counted on to be present when expected and in most cases consists of students who want to be there to learn something. This debating can all be a good deal of fun as well as a great learning experience.

Debating in Other Courses

Debate can likewise be a stimulating addition to any other course you are taking or teaching, such as government, science, or literature. It doesn't have to be a communication course. Have you ever tried arguing about the "big bang" theory? There are plenty of potential topics in a history class. Should America have declared its independence? Was slavery the main cause of the Civil War? Or in literature, was Hamlet a wimp?

In such a class you're going to be reading up on the subject of controversy anyway, and debate tends to generate even more research than usual. You aren't in this case trying to learn about debate itself, but you will learn a good deal more about the issues relevant to that course.

Once more, the key to transforming a class into an arena for audience debate is to treat the group as deliberating together on controversial issues and then to utilize the formats and methods we'll be describing later on.

Outside of the Classroom

Audiences assemble for all kinds of occasions in an educational institution. For instance, at most institutions there are convocations or assemblies where programs are presented, a natural situation for a public debate. This is another source of audiences, a sitting duck.

Beyond regularly scheduled convocations, there are plenty of other occasions when students and others are led to assemble, ripe for an audience debate. Themes for special occasions abound: Free Enterprise Day, Black Awareness Week, the Nuclear Weapons Symposium, and many more. Not all of the sponsors of such events are anxious to have debates, but some of them are, and relevant topics easily emerge for these ready-made audiences. For example, the Pre-Law Club on many campuses has meetings at which debate is welcomed and usually a number of the members are on the debate squad anyway, so the talent is there.

The arrival of folks from off of a college campus is generally the impetus for more meetings, assemblies, and programs. One campus has a regularly planned debate on the institution's alumni week end, with alumni debaters taking speaking roles along with the students. Another campus has an annual Parents' Day Debate, entertaining a team from a nearby school as opponents, and locating the event in the flowery campus courtyard where folding chairs are set up and passersby are often attracted to listen in. The students have to take their parents to something. And recall also that audience debate by definition calls for full participation of the audience members through questions, speeches, and voting, so the additional participation of knowledgeable and caring alumni or parents can add a great deal of vigor and challenge to these events. Just try debating a universal military draft on such an occasion.

A Debating Society

One way to put together the group you need for audience debating on a regular basis is to form a debating society at your school (if you don't yet have one). The Oxford Union has been in existence as a debating society for centuries. Some others don't last quite that long. Usually the people who come together in such a society are looking for experience in intellectual disputation and are highly interested in public affairs and current events. Among the advantages are the fact that there is a regular membership list, at least some of whom may be counted upon to attend the debates, and that through repeated experience the people who come together know what they are doing and generally become more competent and skillful at debating.

If you as a sponsor or organizer decide to promote a debating society in order to have a regular audience, it is best to be methodical about your procedure. Rules of procedure for debates can be standardized, with leeway for experimentation, so that members will know what to expect. You'll find more about setting up a debating society in Chapter 13. Such a society can provide a reliable, well-trained audience for regular debating by persons who enjoy and profit from it.

Hang Out Your Shingle

Another important way to assemble people for public debates is to schedule a debate just like any other public occasion. You can put together a package consisting of an attractive topic, a suitable location, and some able speakers, publicize the whole thing, and wait for the throng to arrive.

This is an exceptionally practical enterprise on most college campuses and can also be accomplished readily by other adult educational organizations. People are used to having programs to go to. Sponsorship by a teacher, a forensics organization, or an academic department is usually sufficient to provide access to an appropriate room or auditorium. In a typical case, a campus forensics union would decide to schedule a public debate and would make the arrangements and serve as the sponsoring organization.

Of course, the throng may not come. There have been public debates where no one showed up at all, so be ready for some disappointments. Chapter 13 will give you specific directions for advertising and administering public debate programs of this kind.

You can sponsor more than one debate, of course (and we hope that you will). A series of debates may be scheduled, each building upon the others. A campus forum, which has regularly scheduled debates, has been established in many schools, with a sponsoring organization responsible for various aspects of the series. Once established, such a forum often develops a life of its own, attracting regular participants because it is well known already.

If a public debating program is at all extensive, systematic audience building must be incorporated into its functions. It is a matter of experience that many people who have attended a debate for the first time enjoy the event much more than they expected to and leave asking, "When is the next debate?" It's nice to have an answer to that one.

So sponsoring one or more public debates is one more way of providing opportunities for participation right here at home.

GOING OFF YOUR TURF

Differences of opinion are what make debates and horse races, so going off the campus or outside the boundaries of your own class or club will give added richness and variety to your debating experience. When a community member speaks up to tell a school debater, "Kid, you don't know what you're talking about," this tends to make the kid sit up and take notice. Life can also get interesting when the school debater (politely) tells the bank president that he doesn't know what he's talking about, either. There are places, then, where you can reach challenging audiences beyond your own "turf."

Clubs and Organizations

The main alternative to creating audiences in your own bailiwick is to go out and find audiences which already exist elsewhere. Fortunately, in any community there are scads of clubs and organizations which are actively seeking good programs for their meetings. For instance, service clubs such as the Rotary and Optimists generally hold weekly meetings and encompass a broad range of interests. Business and professional clubs, social fellowships, sororities, and a multitude of special interest organizations ranging from garden clubs to computer societies provide additional golden opportunities for public debating.

With an established program and a group of debaters who like to do this sort of thing (it gets in your blood a little), you can even begin to take "commissions" from those who would like to order a certain debate topic. For example, a parent-teachers group at one high school, where there was a heated dispute concerning whether to maintain an affiliation with the national Parent Teachers Association, invited a nearby college to provide a relatively objective debate on the subject to try to clarify the issues. In such a case they come to you.

Once more we invite you to turn to chapter 13 for more details on setting up a debate speakers bureau.

Going on Tour

Stretching ourselves out geographically, we may find a variety of audience situations by sending a team on "tour" to other parts of the state or country.

Some schools and groups send out a team to debate against teams located at a series of other institutions, as when teams from Harvard or Oxford Universities make public appearances at various schools. You might well send out a couple of teams of your own who then agree to appear before different organizations (such as alumni clubs) away from the school campus.

The logistical hazards, we might note, ranging from missed connections to severe winter storms, are considerable in planning and executing a tour, but you do gain the advantages of a greater range of audiences as well as fringe benefits which come from the travel itself.

Use the Broadcast Media

The electronic media appear to be with us to stay. Although the measured audiences for media debates are hardly overwhelming, the potential is there for audiences exceeding what you might find back in the auditorium. Televised Presidential debates and such debate-style programs as "Firing Line" and the MacNeil/Lehrer NewsHour suggest that some viewers enjoy public controversy.

On a more modest scale, opportunities are provided by the campus radio or TV stations, the local educational channel, and cable systems looking for public affairs programming. Arrangements may be subject to considerable negotiation and formats must be carefully tailored to the medium being used.

Although mass media debates make audience participation of a direct sort more difficult, you can look into the possibilities of "call-in" features as well as measuring audience opinions through call-in or mail responses. Don't hold your breath when you do this, though. Stimulating delayed audience feedback is a gradual process, too.

FINDING PRINCIPAL SPEAKERS

Keeping in mind the fact that in public debate we have to think of everyone present as a participant, we want to look now at those participants who take on the special responsibilities of "principal speakers." They're the ones who start the debate off, make sure that important substantive issues are treated, and summarize appropriately at the end.

The individuals who take on these key roles as principal speakers may be recruited from a wide range of sources. There are no eligibility rules in audience debate; anyone may play.

Your Own Cadre

First of all, if you are the one who is selecting principal speakers for a debate, you can pick from your own crew, if you have a crew. Indeed, if you are conducting very much audience debating, you should begin to have a pool of persons who are experienced, able, and reliable. Optimally they are organized into a squad, society, club, or class. Naturally, when you are having debates within your own argumentation and debate class or within your debating society, you can rotate assignments and give everyone a chance to be a principal speaker.

Not everyone is equally good at audience debate. In going out into the general public you face a good deal of public accountability in this activity and demands for high quality performance are sometimes intense, so you will want to deal with speakers you can count on to be effective in the debate. When you develop your own cadre of potential debaters, you can begin to incorporate practice, observation, and critiques into the nourishment of talent for future debates.

In selecting the principal speakers for a particular debate, you can choose among those who are most interested in or prepared for the topic (or willing to prepare), and who would be most effective for the audience which the team will be facing. You refrain from assigning someone to a side in violation of his or her personal convictions.

One method for selecting principal speakers is to have formal "try-outs," when anyone who wants to debate will have a chance to be picked. The try-outs should be conducted to find out whether the prospective speaker is prepared and can adapt readily to the audience and the demands of arguing coherently.

Not everyone in the debate needs to come from your class or "in" group, of course. There are other individuals who may be available and whose abilities you have observed, including those who have participated in debates as audience members. Persons who have special competence or interests may be invited to take part even in a classroom debate. For instance, if the debate revolves around an up-coming election, Young Democrats, Campus Republicans, or Young Libertarians may be eager to send representatives. At other times, to help draw an audience, you may call upon a popular team captain or campus politico. The editor of the student paper or news director of your station may want to speak about a freedom of the press issue.

If you yourself are a student trying to figure out whether to get further involved, then attend and participate in scheduled debates. Take a class, if you're not doing so now. Join the debate society or team. In this arena, as in so many others, there's plenty of room at the top.

Debaters from Other Schools

A new dimension may be added to a campus debate if the two sides are represented by students from different schools. The tradition of interscholastic competition is well established at both the high school and college levels, and audiences may be attracted and stimulated by that   factor. Furthermore, new and better arguments sometimes come   into the discussion when the constructive speakers are from different schools. In some debate programs, the main portion of the audience debating schedule consists of such interscholastic engagements.

Earlier we suggested that you might take a tour. Now the shoe may be on the other foot and somebody else taking a tour can help to provide principal speakers for your debate. Especially attractive for colleges are the touring debaters from Great Britain, Australia, Japan, and even Russia who are invited to the United States each year to engage in debates under the auspices of the Speech Communication Association.

On occasion invitations may be issued to other schools on the basis of the nature of the other institution itself. A liberal arts college might get representatives of an engineering school to debate genetic engineering, nuclear safety, or even the value of a liberal arts education.

A degree of care should be exercised in some cases to ensure that the element of school rivalry does not unduly overshadow the argumentative clash on substantive issues. You also, after a while, get some idea of which schools are likely to send debaters well qualified for public debating and which are not. The attractiveness of your own program, after all, depends upon the quality of the debaters who take part, wherever they come from.

And one other thing. Explicit attention must be given to the sometimes complex arrangements for such debates, which are to be discussed in more detail in good old Chapter 13.

Experts

Remember also that we do not have to stick to students or

members of our own organization for participants in public debating. No matter how well prepared the students are, the debate may benefit from the inclusion of interested and knowledgeable individuals from all walks of life.

A basic tenet of audience debate is the comparison and mutual testing of competing arguments. When eligibility rules and their equivalents are no longer relevant, the speakers may include teachers, graduate students, community members, or anybody else. A debate on the campus issue of whether a certain university should continue its investments in anti-environmental enterprises, for instance, might draw upon faculty and administration members who are actively dealing with the issue. We should keep our eyes open for townspeople and parents who might be willing to take part, too.

Recognized experts on any subject can make a valuable contribution to the debate and sometimes make the whole occasion more meaningful and attractive. You can invite subject matter experts to be principal speakers and you may welcome their contributions whenever they are members of the audience. You will find a certain amount of diplomacy useful in making arrangements when they involve outside experts who have been invited to the campus. For instance, you might pair a student with an expert as principal speakers on both sides rather than opposing student speakers to experts. Often enough you may sponsor a debate in which authorities simply debate each other, with the student body's role limited to asking questions and expressing opinions. In every case our goal is to have a meaningful and challenging debate.

A provision for broad and active participation has to be an objective in public argument, where the rationality of lines of argument and of social decision-making is ultimately measured in accordance with the adherence of critical audiences.

Chapter 3

Formats for Public Debates

Public debates come in all shapes and sizes. There simply is no single established format for audience debates to follow, so you're on your own when it comes to deciding the number and order of the speeches you're going to have, the amount and kind of audience participation, and the time limits to be imposed. How the debate is to be structured will depend in each case on the immediate circumstances, ranging from the nature of the topic and the audience to the total amount of time which will be available. There are plenty of format options you can incorporate when you are setting up a such a debate.

Let's take a look at a format which has proven popular for classroom debates. As you can see, it fits easily within a 50-minute class period.

First affirmative speech	5 minutes
First negative speech	5 minutes
Second affirmative speech	5 minutes
Second negative speech	5 minutes
Audience speeches (2 minutes each)	20 minutes
Negative summary	3 minutes
Affirmative summary	3 minutes
Audience vote	

In the above format, each side is represented by two principal speakers. The four 5-minute "constructive" speeches allow the speakers to present the major contentions upon which their positions rest, including some evidence and reasoning to support these contentions, as well as to begin to answer what the other side is saying. Since this is a classroom debate, a substantial period has been allotted to gaining maximum audience involvement through allowing audience members to ask questions and make speeches of their own. Brief summary periods (following a tradition of allowing the affirmative to have the first and last "say") permit two of the principal speakers to tie together the main threads of argument which they would like to reinforce. The popular vote at the end requires everyone in the class to try to decided which position he or she is supporting as the debate ends.

Your class may use this format to debate almost any imaginable controversial topic. Try it. You'll like it.

Sometimes in a class or in other situations you'll have more time available for the debate. At the end of this chapter you'll find a sample program for an evening debate designed for a period of an hour and a half or so. And sometimes you'll have less time available. Suppose you are invited to present a debate at a noon service club meeting where the time allotted for the program may by as little as 20 minutes. The same format might be suitable for a radio or television appearance, where programming tends to be divided into 30-minute segments. Here's a possibility.

First affirmative speaker	5 minutes
First negative speaker	5 minutes
First affirmative cross-examined	
by second negative	3 minutes
First negative cross-examined	
by second affirmative	3 minutes
Second negative summary	4 minutes
Second affirmative summary	4 minutes
Audience vote	

This format provides for only one constructive speech on each side and permits no direct audience participation at all. It does add an interaction component in the form of cross-examination conducted by the principal speakers themselves. The audience still votes at the end. You may, of course, try out this format in a class or club meeting, too.

The format for a debate may be strikingly complex at times. You've seen the nationally televised debates between Presidential candidates, for instance; they are undoubtedly the most widely watched public debates we have. The complicated formats for these debates are arrived at through intense negotiations among representatives of the candidates, the television networks, and the sponsoring organization.

The Cleveland debate in 1980 between candidates Jimmy Carter and Ronald Reagan is a case in point. In this debate, sponsored by the League of Women Voters, the cast of characters included not only the two candidates and a moderator, but also four journalists who serve as panelists. The use of a panel of questioners has become something of a norm in televised political debates. We aren't recommending the procedure for much audience debating, but, as we will see, it does constitute one of your many options.

The panelists in the Carter-Reagan debate, during the first half of the televised program, would each ask a question, the same question, to the two candidates in turn. After the candidates had answered that one, the panelist would ask a "follow-up" question. Finally, during this phase of the debate, each candidate was permitted a short rebuttal speech.

For the second half of the 1980 debate, moderator Howard K. Smith felt obliged to say about the procedural rules, "It's quite simple; they're only complicated when I explain them." In this case there were no follow-up questions, but each candidate was given two opportunities to follow up on what he or his opponent had said about the question which was posed. The panelists still had the role of setting forth the basic question to be answered. Finally, at the end of the broadcast, each candidate was allotted three minutes for a "closing statement."

Many factors contributed to the complexity of the format. Because the debate was a nationally televised media event, not only was the total time to be kept within an exact limitation, but also no speech was to be longer than three minutes in order to keep the kind of fast pace which viewers had come to expect in public affairs broadcasting. Because the debate was a "news" event, the issues were to be set by persons other than the candidates themselves. Many of the other rules were a product of the effort by both candidates to get an advantage of some kind or prevent an advantage to the other side.

Much of the time you won't have national television to contend with, though, so much simpler formats will suffice, depending on circumstances. The idea, then, is to consider the various options open to you in setting up the format of a debate. The rest of this chapter is intended to show you, not how a debate must be set up, but the many ways you can arrange it. In each case, attention should be given to the aim of the debate, the subject matter, and the circumstances under which the debate is to be presented.

TIME LIMITS

How long should a debate be? How long should anyone be allowed to talk? The most conspicuous control on the flow of any debate is the imposition of time limits on the speakers, and in this matter you still have a great many options.

For instance, no inherent limit exists on the total length of time a debate should take. The famous Lincoln-Douglas debates were three hours in length; debates in the United States Senate may go on for days and days. On the other hand, you can have a mini-debate, on the model of the "Point/Counterpoint" segments you might have seen parodied on late-night TV, which takes less than five minutes in its entirety.

Most audience debates these days are designed with formats which take somewhere between 30 minutes and two hours. It all depends on the situation. The shorter forms, as illustrated earlier, may be dictated by the half hour or so allotted for a television production or luncheon club program. Classroom debates or school assemblies and convocations may have to stop when the bell rings. An evening program or class may be longer, allowing the relative leisure of an hour and a half or two hours for fuller participation and deliberation. With more flexibility, some sets of rules, such as parliamentary procedure, provide for the audience itself to decide for themselves when they have had enough and vote to close the debate at any time.

The several component parts of the debate may also be allotted varying amounts of time. Depending upon the aim of the occasion, different proportions of time may be devoted to constructive and rebuttal speeches, to cross-examination, and to audience participation. The allowance for audience participation time may be more flexible than the others, perhaps. If the audience doesn't want to participate much, the period will necessarily be shorter; if they are eager to take part, that portion of the format may sometimes be extended.

Options also exist with respect to the length of each speech. Opening constructive speeches may be of any length you want, although eight to ten minutes is fairly standard. Rebuttal and summary speeches tend to run shorter. In a sample format given earlier, the constructive speeches were five minutes in length and the summaries (one to a side) were three minutes. The time limit for speeches by audience members usually is even shorter, two or three minutes being the standard. Under some sets of rules, speakers may yield part of their time to other members in order to get questions answered or for other purposes, meaning that in effect two persons share a time allotment.

Here's another possibility. When the audience has been encouraged to ask questions of a speaker, a "double clock" may be used, one to keep track of constructive time and the other to allocate question-answering time. Thus, in one sample format given at the end of this chapter, the speaker is given eight minutes on one clock and a maximum of six minutes on the question clock, so that if questions are abundant he or she will have 14 minutes of platform time.

It goes without saying that common notions of fairness lead to the expectation that each side in a controversy will be given equal amounts of time, even though there might be circumstances under which, say, an unfamiliar or unpopular position might well require

extra time to explain or defend. In any case, you will want to keep
norms and expectations in mind while remaining ready to adapt even
time limits to the needs of the audience and the situation.

CONSTRUCTIVE AND REBUTTAL SPEECHES

In keeping with the basic aim of public argument, namely the
facilitation of rational and informed decision making, any debate may
be expected to expose the main arguments and evidence upon which
the decisions may be based. Relatively formal "constructive" and
"rebuttal" speeches presented by affirmative and negative debaters
have traditionally served this function by setting forth the contentions
on each side in a systematic and coherent manner. A "debate" is
sometimes thought of as composed entirely of such speeches.

We may have implied so far that the sides in a public debate are
defended by two-person "teams." Naturally, when you stop to think
about it, there is no overwhelming reason why a side cannot be
defended by just one individual, or by three or four person teams.
Even with a two-person unit, we already suggested in the "short"
format above that there may be time for only one constructive speech
on each side. And with a very familiar topic, you may want to
experiment with starting a debate without any constructive speeches
at all. Just start from scratch with audience participation.

But let's see about these longer speeches.

Constructive Speeches. In the format examples given
previously, the designation of "first affirmative," "first negative," etc.,
referred to constructive speeches. If you assume the responsibility
for giving a constructive speech, you will be expected to inform or
remind the audience of the arguments on your side of the proposition
and, in effect, to present a case for your position. Most audiences
expect negative as well as affirmative speakers to give them a well-
prepared case on the proposition, with reasoning and evidence to
support their contentions. We'll talk about case construction later,
but for the moment a case may be thought of as any well-thought-out
set of arguments.

You can and probably should also engage in some refutation
during your constructive speech, answering points made by the other

side. Pointing out apparent weaknesses in the arguments presented by their speakers as well as "rebuilding" your own arguments in response to their attacks produces the necessary clash in a debate and guides the audience through the complexities of the matter in controversy. To rely entirely upon refutation, as negative speakers sometimes do, may violate the needs and expectations of the audience as much as completely ignoring the presence of the opposition tends to do.

A rather different species of pre-planned speech which is occasionally used in audience debating is a preliminary and presumably factual or historical account of the controversy presented by a third party before the advocates start firing. Such a practice may be useful when the audience needs background information before they can begin considering formal arguments. Impartial fact-finding is extremely difficult, however, and our observation is that this procedure does not work very well.

Rebuttals. The rebuttal or summary (we're inclined to prefer the term "summary") speeches in an audience debate give each side opportunities to select major issues that have emerged as well as to respond to points made by opposition members and the audience before the final vote is taken. If there has been an open forum period, the summary speeches will normally follow it and conclude the debate.

You may be aware of the tournament debating convention through which the affirmative side is allowed to give both the first and the last speech, a practice which is represented in the sample formats above. This convention may have some relevance for policy propositions or as a kind of fairness, but most audiences are not familiar with it, and such a practice remains an open option, In an audience debate you may put the summary speeches in any order you wish.

The duties associated with speaker positions which have become norms in tournament debating apply much less rigorously before audiences. Your main responsibility is to see that important arguments get presented, and at appropriate times. Having the "plan" in the first affirmative speech or saving plan attacks for the second negative may at times be good ideas, but such conventions may well be ignored at other times. Even such "rules" as permitting no new arguments in rebuttal speeches are not rules in audience debate. If you don't think of it until late, go ahead and give it. The audience may be wary of them, but they are entitled to any good argument at any time.

Cross-Examination. The designated debaters may interact with one another in less discursive ways as well. They don't necessarily merely give speeches.

The basic form of such interaction is a cross-examination procedure. A period of cross-examination may be built into the format. Most typically, in such a period, one of the affirmative speakers cross-examines the negative speaker after his or her speech is over, or the negative cross-examines the affirmative. This procedure is familiar in tournament debating. The time is assumed to belong to the questioner, and ground rules would provide that this period should be used for relatively short questions rather than for an additional speech. Such a period may be placed after each speech in the debate or after certain ones, say the two opening speeches.

For an even more open cross-examination procedure, either speaker of the opposition may be permitted to ask questions, or a sort of free-for-all may even be arranged in which the two (or more) members of one side ask questions of the other side as a group. This is not as hazardous as it sounds.

AUDIENCE PARTICIPATION

The audience as at the heart of audience debating, of course. Although we assume that the real locus of the debate is in every case the minds of the audience members, their active participation is an element to be built into your format wherever possible.

Among the many format options available in setting up a public debate are a number which provide means for listeners to become speakers and thus to interact directly with the debaters and with one another.

One reasonable devise to incorporate is a forum period in which the debate is opened up for audience members to participate. The simplest method is to allow anyone to say anything. Thus the remarks may in some cases by relatively formal speeches, in which the members come forward and speak from the platform or, of they prefer, from their spots in the audience. Such speeches may be on either side of the proposition. Normally the rules will call for alternating speeches on either side or for the chair to call on the sides alternately, but where there are more speakers who want to talk on one side than there are on the other, an imbalance may yet occur. There will also be speakers who rise to say, "I don't know which side this comment is on," so you will have some unclassified entries as well.

During floor debate, anyone is free to continue consideration of arguments that have been advanced in the constructive speeches or bring up brand new arguments to be considered.

An interesting variation in the format is to partition the floor debate so that part of it comes relatively early in the program, to be followed by further constructive speaking and later yet another forum period for audience participation.

Audience Questions. Since audiences are used to having "question periods" after formal speeches, the participants will frequently be inclined to stick to asking questions of the debaters rather than giving opinions of their own. The chair may wish to make it clear that the forum period is not limited to questions, unless indeed you wish to make such a limitation a ground rule. Persons are granted the floor for a specified period of time, frequently for two minutes, so anyone with a question may ask it and then yield the remainder of his or her time to the other person for answering. When the two minutes have elapsed, another member from the floor is called upon.

Questions from the audience do not necessarily need to be limited to a special time set aside for them. The constructive speakers may be questions directly as they speak, and the rules will generally establish ways in which this can be done. When permitted under the rules, a member of the audience may simply arise and ask, through the chair, whether the speaker will "yield" to a question. The chair then asks the speaker whether he or she will yield and, if so, the person asks the question and the speaker tries to answer it. As suggested under the time limits, you may want to establish a second clock to keep track of this aspect of the debate.

Where the audience as very large, and random questions bothersome or difficult to manage, you may choose to follow the example of the Presidential debates and have delegated representatives on the platform who will set forth what everybody wants to know and doesn't have a chance to ask. A variation on this technique is to request written permission and have the representatives sort through them and pose the best or most numerous ones to the speakers. Furthermore, if your debate is conducted on radio or television, you will find that the technology for call-in questions and other interactive techniques is becoming increasingly available.

Heckling.   One dramatic and colorful form of audience participation is direct heckling of the speakers. In some groups, such as the British Parliament, heckling is a common and expected practice; in others it much be overtly encouraged. Heckling is a form of direct and immediate feedback, and as such may indeed be quite useful in countering bombast and developing responsiveness in the speakers.

There will be times, though, when this practice will merely add to the bombast or will be unduly distracting. Some hecklers are too crude, too ignorant, or too exhibitionistic to add constructively to the ongoing process of the debate.

In deciding whether to encourage heckling, you will also have to consider the expectation and mores of the audience you are dealing with. In our culture there is quite a bit of respect, even applause, accorded to speakers whether they deserve it or not, and heckling will therefore be regarded by many listeners as automatically boorish or impolite.

Still, in your class or debating society you should give it a try, both to see its attractions and to learn how to deal with heckling when it occurs.

Voting.   In arranging for audience participation, you will not want to ignore the act of voting. Voting is not exactly speaking, but it is an important expression of audience attitudes. Even if you should choose not to conduct any kind of formal audience vote as part of your format, you might well have a statement made to the effect that each audience member should make his or her own decision.

More formally, however, a direct vote may be taken on the merits of the question at the end of the debate. Most commonly this would consist of a voice vote. "All in favor say aye," etc. In a close contest, a hand or standing vote may be appropriate, and sometimes you may have your rules suggest the possibility of the motion called in parliamentary procedure a "division of the assembly," in which a close voice vote may be formally transformed into a counted vote. Occasionally even written ballots may be appropriate.

One interesting variant, following the procedures of the British Oxford and Cambridge Debating Societies, is to have the audience leave by separate doors, depending upon which side they favor , with tellers keeping track of the actual count.

OFFICERS AND RULES

Implied in many of the format choices we have talked about is the presence of a presiding officer, one of a number of possible officials who might be assigned to an audience debate. Besides the chairperson, moderator, or "speaker of the assembly," there could be a timekeeper to keep time, a recorder or clerk to keep track of motions or perhaps the arguments themselves, a sergeant-at-arms or equivalent for ceremonial purposes or actually to keep order. a parliamentarian, and ushers to hand out programs and help instruct audience members about their roles.

The chair, of course, has a key role, and we'll talk about this later. Basically, he or she is called upon to keep the procedure orderly, to remain impartial, and to recognize and introduce people at appropriate times. But also, this position involves maintaining a "bedside manner" which will encourage debate and help the audience members to be receptive and reflective. Furthermore, the chair may well have some instructional responsibilities, to tell people what the rules are and how to carry out a profitable deliberation of the question at hand.

Whether or not you have officers other than a chair depends upon the nature and formality of the situation. In some cases the chair can carry out all of the necessary roles, even time-keeping. In a parliamentary assembly, a recorder or secretary may be necessary to keep a full record of the proceedings; in a public debate where the proposition is not being modified in any way, this would not be necessary.

The format may also make allowance for a representative of a sponsoring or supporting organization to take ceremonial roles such as introducing the group who are going to debate or thanking the participants.

Rules. Debate being a formal activity, some rules are always necessary, and since the audience members are involved as participants in one way or another, these rules must be communicated to them.

The best known set of rules by which debate is conducted is *Robert's Rules of Order.* These rules are designed for circumstances in which disagreement may be strenuous and modification of propositions is possible. Familiarity with these rules is useful to any debater, but for most purposes the kind of public debate we are exploring does not call for such complex rules.

Most frequently, a brief page or so of rules for the particular event will be sufficient. This page may provide information on the time limits and order of speaking, procedures for entering the debate and asking questions, provisions for cross-examination and heckling, possible incidental motions such as points of personal privilege, seating arrangements, means of closing debate, and voting procedures.

Sample sets of rules from actual intercollegiate public debates are appended at the end of this chapter and you can examine for yourself their constituent parts. One set has been employed successfully for a number of years as a large state university for debates which sometimes attract hundreds of audience members, and the other is for an evening debate sponsored by the debating societies of two smaller liberal arts institutions. You can see the various options which have been chosen by the sponsors of these evening debates. They include such things as constructive and summary speeches, yielding for questions, double clocks, encouragement of heckling, a prescribed seating arrangement, means of recognition, a procedure for closing debate by popular vote, and voting procedures on the resolution itself.

The set of rules, then, in effect summarizes the choices you have made in developing the format for a debate. We're ready to look at the opportunities you'll have for participation and then figure out what you'll be debating about.

The Illini Forensic Association

RULES OF DEBATE

1. **Seating**: Members of the House will seat themselves according to their sentiments on the resolution -- those <u>for</u> the resolution on the Chair's right (as the Chair faces the audience), those <u>against</u> the resolution on the Chair's left, and those <u>undecided</u> in the center section. Members of the House may cross the floor as their opinions change.

2. **The Resolution**: The Main Motion before the House (the debate resolution) may not be amended.

4. **Heckling**: Heckling is encouraged, but its use will be under the Chair's strict supervision. Witty, intelligent, and clever heckling is permitted; dull, tactless, and boorish heckling simply will not occur. Members who violate this rule will be asked to leave.

4. **Principal Speakers**: There will be four principal speeches, after which general debate is in order.
   a. The first speaker will introduce the resolution and <u>is not</u> available for questions from the floor during his or her 8-minute speech.
   2. An opposing speaker will deliver an 8-minute speech during which he or she <u>is not</u> available for "points of information" (questions).
   3. An 8-minute speech follows by the side supporting the resolution. This speaker <u>is available</u> for "points of information" (questions).
   4. An opposing speaker will deliver an 8-minute speech during which he or she <u>is available</u> for "points of information" (questions).

5. **Asking Questions**. When members of the House wish to ask a question (a point of information) of a speaker they may do so by standing up and asking: "Will the speaker yield for a question?" During the principal speeches members are asked to limit themselves to one question each time they rise.

RULES OF DEBATE (Cont.)

6. **Answering Questions:** During the principal speeches, the speaker may refuse to yield the floor for a question. When a principal speaker yields to a question, his or her answer is not counted against the 8-minute time limit on his/her speech until 6 minutes have been consumed in answering questions. Thus, the third and fourth principal speakers may each have a maximum of 14 minutes.

7. **The General Debate Period:** After the four principal speeches, the Chair will recognize members of the House for speeches, comments, and questions. When recognized by the Chair, a member will have the floor for a maximum of three minutes. These speakers will be recognized alternately for and against the resolution. Preference will be given to members who have not previously spoken.

8. **Ending Debate:** Debate may be ended by general consent (if no member wishes to speak) or by a motion to end debate. The proper form is: "I move to end debate." The motion requires a two-thirds vote. Upon passage of a motion to end debate, a principal speaker against and a principal speaker for the resolution will each have four minutes for a summary speech. The summary speeches are not subject to questions.

9. **Adjournment** The motion to adjourn is not in order until the House has voted on the resolution.

10. **Robert's Rules:** Any matter not covered by these special rules will be decided by the Chair and House Parliamentarian in accordance with *Robert's Rules of Order* (Newly Revised).

MONON BELL DEBATE   **MONDAY, NOVEMBER 8, 1993**
8:00 P.M.   **ROOM 106. EAST COLLEGE**

Topic: Resolved, that this house believes that family values are
          deteriorating because the hand that rocks the cradle is
          preoccupied

    1st Affirmative   Bryan Boyce, Wabash College
    1st Negative   Aaron Lucchetti, DePauw University
    2nd Affirmative   C. Lee Hill, Jr., Wabash College
    2nd Negative   Tricia Robinson, DePauw University
    Moderator   Kathy Lester

<u>Rules</u>

This is a parliamentary debate. Audience participation will be encouraged, and even "heckling" within reason is permitted.

Each of the above speakers will have up to eight minutes of uninterrupted speaking.

After the conclusion of the second negative speech, the floor will be open for any members of the audience to speak.

The Moderator will limit speeches from the floor to two minutes each and will attempt to alternate speeches from each side.

At the expiration of the period for debate from the floor, the Moderator will recognize each side for a five-minute closing statement.

The debate will conclude with a rising vote on the resolution.

Chapter 4

Audience Members as Participants

Everyone is important at a public debate. Even if you are "just" an audience member, which is what you'll be most of the time, your presence is the central fact in a public debate. The whole point of the enterprise is to create or increase the adherence of an audience (that's you) to propositions presented for your assent.

Whenever you attend a debate, you may find a number of functions available to you.

Decision Maker. As an audience member you will almost always be called upon to arrive at some conclusion as to which side of the proposition you agree with. Frequently you will express this conclusion as a vote. Since the thinking you do in your own mind and the preference you ultimately express are the object of all of the rational influence being exerted by the speakers, you have a lot of power there, as well as a responsibility to think and vote as reasonably as you can. That's important.

Advocate. A certain proportion of the audience may be rooting for one side or the other, may have a substantial commitment before the debate even begins, and you may be one of these. That's all right. If you have a conviction and reasons to support it, participating as an audience member gives you a chance to express your opinion and try to influence other people as much as the speakers who are formally assigned to do so.

Facilitator. A third function which audience members serve is facilitating rational judgment by raising fresh points, seeking clarification, or focusing issues. They try to make sure that all of the bases are covered In some formats facilitating is the primary responsibility of certain members of the audience and in others, where the ultimate decision is to be made by a delegated agency, it may be the main function of the bulk of the listeners.

All of the Above. Most persons will have at least a "leaning" which may make them advocates to some extent. Furthermore, most persons, even if they are very partisan, have some desire to be rational decision makers and listen to what the other side says. And everyone is to a degree concerned with facilitating the discussion. Therefore, the above functions are not necessarily exclusive. You can do it all.

Negative Functions. Not everyone at a public debate will be constructively engaged in it. There will probably be "innocent by-standers," for instance. They just came with a friend, they are in a required course where debates are held, or they may be a photographer on assignment for the local newspaper. If you happen to be one of these, keep your ears open anyway. Don't be an ignorant bystander. You might learn something. Worse yet, at a debate there may also be deliberate "disrupters." They may regard the debate as stupid or they merely want to get it over with for personal reasons. Or they may even be completely opposed to having a certain matter talked about at all. An awareness of mixed motives of all participants may be useful to you in understanding what is going on.

WHAT DO YOU DO?

Now what actually happens when you join the audience at a public debate? What are you supposed to know and do? What will be expected of you? What are some of the specific options you have if you want to participate directly? We'll take a special look at four aspects of audience participation, namely the procedures and decorum in public debating, asking questions, making a speech of your own, and the fascinating phenomenon of "heckling." Then we'll also consider the possibility that you might eventually agree to be a "principal speaker" or that some time you might be the chairperson at the meeting.

Procedures and Decorum

In the first place, you've been in plenty of audiences in your life, and the general norms which apply to such situations are suitable enough for public debates. Just go in and have a seat. And be reasonably polite.

But there's often more to it.

It is important for you to know what special rules of debate are in effect. If the debate is part of the meeting of a club or class which meets regularly, you are probably well enough aware of what these rules are. At other times and when a large crowd is expected, you may find ushers handing out written copies of the formal rules for that particular debate, as illustrated in Chapter 3. You might need to know right away, for instance, that those favorable to the resolution are expected to sit on the chairperson's right as he or she faces the audience and those opposed sit on the left side. You'll also want to know such things as the time limits, how to get recognized if you want to say something, and when the debate will be over.

As for what you do after you have found a seat, you don't necessarily have to move a muscle. You can content yourself with being a listener. Even then, though, remember that there will ordinarily be a debate going on in your own mind as you personally try to think about what is being said and make a decision about which side you agree with.

But then maybe you do want to move a muscle. One very basic concept in communication is "feedback," a process which allows a sender to adjust a message to the responses of the receivers. As a listener you can provide speakers with helpful feedback through a wide assortment of nonverbal channels. You can look at the speaker approvingly, you can nod your head, or you can scowl. You can applaud, or laugh, or hiss and boo. These are normal enough audience responses and not at all out of line at a debate. Recall that the basic objective of public debate is to arrive at rational decisions collectively. As an audience member you join in this process, even without saying anything, if you encourage strong arguments and dismiss weak or irrelevant ones through the nonverbal feedback you provide. Your "crowd noises" can promote rationality.

Since communication is inherently a social enterprise, your interaction with other audience members has significance as well. Audience members influence one another. For instance, when some listeners applaud, the speaker is not the only one affected, so in giving feedback you are in effect communicating with everyone. If you wish to go beyond nonverbal indications of your attitude, you may even express yourself verbally, in words, to your fellow members of the audience. You can whisper to a neighbor. You can make audible comments. You can write little notes. Sometimes you'll have a great idea and will try to get your friend to stand up and speak about it. In a lively debate, there is a great deal of this co-communication taking place throughout the assembly.

At times there may be too much of this "co-communication" going on. It is in the best interest of all members of the audience to be able to hear what is being said and to think seriously about it. The chair will make every effort to keep a degree of order and everyone should be expected to be reasonably civil and polite. As a listener you may find it necessary at times to say "shshsh" and "Will you please pipe down" to your confreres. Nonverbal and verbal signals can serve as social controls and keep the noise level down to a dull roar.

Formal rules may again be involved. In televised political debates, the listeners who are physically present are sometimes required to refrain from overt responses of approval or disapproval. Obey the rules.

In any event, without seeking overt recognition at all, you may still play an active and meaningful part in the debate.

Asking Questions

You may want to ask a direct question.

Now we begin to get into more formal procedures, since there are almost always some rules governing question-asking by listeners in a debate. The chair keeps a certain amount of control over this activity.

When the assembly is small or the procedures less formal, you may at times simply raise your hand and say "I have a question," but the process should still stay under the control of the chair. In many situations you will find that a specified period has been set aside for a designated question period. Or you may be asked to put your questions in writing and pass them forward to persons designated to sort them out before asking them.

When the rules are quite formal, you usually will use what in parliamentary procedure is a "yielding" process. If you want to ask a question while someone else is speaking, for instance, you may rise for recognition and ask the chair, "Will the speaker yield for a question?" This can be addressed to one of the principal speakers or to another audience member who is speaking. The chair then asks the speaker if he or she will indeed yield, and if that person agrees to the request, you can go ahead and ask your question. Another way to use the yield procedure is when you yourself have gained recognition to speak. You may say "I have a question to ask the gentleman from the Motorcyclist Association and will be willing to yield time to him for an answer." The biker doesn't have to take the opportunity you offer him, however. Nobody ever has to answer a question. (But he might get booed -- see above -- for not doing so.)

Questions may be addressed to the assembly at large. "Would someone please explain to me about the 'EMP' that people are talking about?" Or they may be addressed (as they frequently are) to those who have given the principal speeches or to any other individual in the audience.

There are plenty of different kinds of questions you can ask. Their two main functions seem to be (1) a genuine search for information or clarity and (2) a desire to put somebody on the spot. To clarify an argument, you can ask a question starting with something like "Are you saying . . .?" To put someone on the spot, or to reveal a weakness, you might ask a question in the form, "If it is true that . . ., then wouldn't it be possible to conclude . . .?" You could also posit a dilemma, where the person would be asked to pick one of two equally distasteful alternatives. We might note even the possibility of a "friendly" question, where a speaker is in effect reminded to add an important supporting argument or piece of evidence. It happens.

Questions are an important element of public debating, and asking questions is sometimes the most vital function played by the audience members. You'll want to be ready to ask about things that concern you.

Giving Speeches from the Floor

Now you may want to go beyond asking questions and make some points of your own. In most public debate situations you'll have a chance to make a speech if you want to. This puts you right into the heart of the debate.

This is another spot where there will be some rules and norms you have to know about. You almost always have to get "recognized" by the chair, for instance. Sometimes you do this by just raising your hand; in more formal debates you stand and say "Madam Chairman." Occasionally you have to sign up ahead of time in order to be given an opportunity to speak. This may be true, for instance, at a hearing conducted by a governmental agency.

If the rules or norms call for speaking from alternate sides of the proposition, you will be expected to give an affirmative speech if you are following a negative one, or the chair may ask you outright which side you are on. When time limits for speeches from the floor are included in the formal rules, you have to be aware of these.

Furthermore, rules or norms may determine whether you are expected to stand up when you speak and whether you are supposed to go to the front of the room to talk. Even if the rules don't say, other members of the audience or the chair may suggest that you stand up (or sit down) or speak from a spot where you may be easily heard. Sometimes you're supposed to come to the microphone.

Once you have figured out the technical procedures governing how you get the opportunity to speak in the debate, all you have to decide after that is what you're going to say.

There is no reason in the world why you can't prepare for your speech ahead of time, of course. Especially when the topic of debate is a matter which you are really concerned about or one where you have some special knowledge or experience, you may outline a speech and have it ready to present when the opportunity comes. As a knowledgeable audience member, you can add substantially to the quality of the debate.

Whether your speech is prepared ahead of time or is a spontaneous, spur of the moment contribution, it may perform any of six (or more) functions in the debate.

1. **New Argument.** You may be aware of a neglected line of reasoning which you think is important and nobody has yet mentioned. In a debate about adding to the national nuclear missile capability, where the issue has been how the nation could win a nuclear war, you may feel that you should add the observation that, "In a nuclear war, even the country that 'wins' actually loses."

2. **Fresh Data.** In a debate about whether those who serve alcohol should be liable for harms done by their customers, an issue might be whether bartenders can detect inebriation. An audience member may have specific information about the efficacy of training programs for teaching people how to do this. He or she may have been through such training, and thus can bring first hand experience to bear on the question. Whenever you know something that other people don't, you can add to the rational processes of argument by presenting it to the audience.

3. **Make a Correction.** Similarly, if facts that are presented by a speaker are known by you to be wrong, you perform an important function if you provide the audience with more accurate information.

4. **Refute.** The "correction" you make may go beyond the information being presented. You may try to demonstrate that a whole line of argument ought to be rejected by the other audience members. The reasoning which has been presented is bad or there is a great deal of evidence to the contrary on a given point, for instance.

5. **A New Construction.** Sometimes you may want to exert more influence to get everyone in the room to look at the proposition in a new and fresh way. You might say, "We have all been looking at this question as a matter of economics. I think we should look at it from a moral perspective. It seems to me to be a matter of right and wrong, of fairness and justice." Or if you are debating U.S. policies in Latin America, you might offer the thought that "Perhaps we should look at the matter specifically as a Latin American situation rather than as a U.S. domestic issue."

6. **Reinforcement.** Have you ever said to yourself in a conversation, "I don't want to repeat a point that somebody else has

already said"? Well, in a public debate repetition and reinforcement are not bad things to do. The fact that you think a particular point is important and valid is itself evidence for other people that that argument has strength. An argument is valid when people find it valid. Communication among audience members about the strength of various elements of reasoning and evidence is useful in the evaluative process for everyone. Reinforcement thus has a logical function. If you liked what somebody else said, you can say so and repeat it.

These six functions give us some idea of the possibilities for approaches to a speech from the floor. Now, in presenting our ideas, we should keep a couple of "tips" in mind as well.

For one thing, try to focus on one main idea in your speech (even though there will be times when you may go ahead and break that rule and work in a series of different points). The idea is that you may have only one chance to speak and quite possibly will face a stringent time limit, so you will want your remarks to have focus and impact. Give them something to remember you by.

For another thing, watch for feedback. Public debate means thinking on your feet, so you will try to adapt to the responses (those nods and scowls) as much as possible when you talk. If people are not accepting what you say, you can modify it. If they are apparently enthusiastic, you can reinforce it even more.

In ensuing chapters we'll have more suggestions. Remember that in a public debate the audience is working together to come up with a rational decision. As a speaker from the floor, you will be playing a significant part in this process.

Heckling

"Heckling" is regarded as rather impolite by many audiences, so if we want to heckle, or to encourage heckling, in our debates, we have to be a little bit careful about it.

Heckling is a form of immediate feedback. If speakers and other audience members can handle it and keep it within civilized bounds, heckling can make a debate more interesting and even more rational. It's a good way to get rid of empty bombast and irrelevant garbage.

In English and Canadian legislatures, heckling is a standard feature of floor debate.

If you are a member of a debating society or school class, you should give it a try. If anything, American audiences tend to be too polite, so knowing how to heckle constructively could be useful.

Constructive heckling performs the functions of most kinds of feedback. It is used to redirect the line of argument or to indicate flaws in evidence and reasoning. When abused it may be intended to show off one's cleverness or to create embarrassment or confusion in others.

In practice, heckling simply means saying out loud what you are thinking privately. You can say "Will the speaker get to the point?" or "What about people who can't afford it?" Such comments are addressed to the rest of the audience as much as to the speaker, so good heckling often encourages more good heckling.

This means that hecklers can get heckled, too. Since debates are social occasions and heckling is a form of audience participation, a key necessity in heckling is to have the audience on your side. If your heckle is a good one, other people will reinforce it. If it is a poor and unpopular heckle, their sympathies may be more with your target than with you. Responding to heckling in a way which keeps the audience on your side or retains the focus of argument where you want it is a useful skill to develop.

So try it. You'll like it. In any event, when you know how to handle it, heckling adds a spectacularly fresh and lively dimension to any debate.

PRINCIPAL SPEAKERS

So far we have been talking about what you can do when you're an audience member. Sometime, though, you may agree to be one of the principal speakers and to take responsibility for defending one side or the other of the proposition. You're still part of the crowd, of course, a sort of "first among equals." Your opinion will be worth as much as the audience members will allow it to be.

As a principal speaker in a public debate you aren't just putting on a display. You're sharing your ideas with other people and seeking their adherence to these ideas.

There will probably be more rules concerning what the principal speakers do than about the activity of any of the others present. Such things as the order of speaking, time limits, provisions for questions, and the like will apply. For instance, if you are a principal speaker, you will normally have a specific, relatively substantial, amount of time in which you can give a well prepared and well developed affirmative or negative speech.

Your primary obligation is to set the grounds for the debate and to identify for the listeners the strongest possible lines of argument in support of the side you represent. You will develop your speeches more formally and be ready to answer points made by the opposition speakers or by other audience members. Presumably you will know more about the topic and will have done more research than most of these others, too.

What we say in future chapters will give you a good many ideas about how to handle these responsibilities and expectations effectively, so we won't say more about them at this time. The main thing to remember is that in a public debate everyone is sharing in the decision process, and principal speakers are supposed to help make these decisions turn out better.

YOU'RE THE CHAIRPERSON

Somebody has to be chair, so while you're getting into public debate you might as well learn how to preside at a meeting. You may end up with that responsibility some time.

Normally, your main duties will be opening the meeting, presiding over the debate, and taking a vote at the end.

Opening the Debate. As chair you will want to compile a checklist of practical and ceremonial duties to perform before the debate gets started.

You can hope that someone else will see that chairs are in place, programs are distributed, and the microphones are working. You yourself can make sure that the speakers are present and ready.

Your first oral task is usually to welcome the audience and to express appreciation to a sponsoring organization or others who have helped to make the debate possible.

Naturally, before the debate begins, you will also introduce the principal speakers and any "officials" of the debate, such as the timekeeper.

Finally, you will make sure that the audience is aware of the rules of the debate. Either point out the rules which have been distributed in writing or explain orally what rules have been adopted.

Now you're ready for the debate to begin.

Presiding. As you preside over the debate, you will find it necessary to know the rules well, to remain impartial, to facilitate the debating, and to maintain order in the house.

Knowing the rules means being ready to rule upon anything which is out of order, of course, but it also means taking an instructional attitude in letting the audience know what they can do and what they are not supposed to do. You might have to explain to an audience how the "yield" procedure we were talking about before works, for instance. If you are operating under a full set of parliamentary procedure, you have a lot to learn. At the least, be sure to review the rules governing the debate you are chairing.

A chairperson is supposed to remain impartial and fair, of course. This is what an audience expects. Avoid making biased remarks or rulings. If you feel you just have to make a statement favoring one side or the other, "step down" from the chair and let someone else preside while you are making your remarks.

An important part of your job as chair is to facilitate discussion. You need to develop a good "bedside manner." While some audiences are raucous from the word go, many times audience members have a certain reluctance to speak, especially at the beginning of the period. You can encourage them. Since the word "speech" is a bit intimidating to some individuals, you could say "Who would like to make a comment?" rather than "Does anybody want to make a speech?" Notice the positive attitude. Be expectant, and don't nag the audience. "Does anyone have a question?" sometimes breaks the ice. One chairperson said, "Would anyone like to make the point that censorship violates the First Amendment?" An audience member responded with "Yes, I'd like to say that," and this pump-priming operation got things started. Throughout the debate keep an eye open for expressions or movements which indicate that an individual who has not spoken yet would like to say something. And you can decide how loosely to interpret the rules when, for instance, a colloquy develops which is constructive and helpful but may be proceeding without proper recognition. There are times when you would let it run.

And there are times when you wouldn't let it run. One of your responsibilities is to maintain order in the assembly. You can rule people out of order. You can have them expelled from the meeting. Usually a rap of the gavel will restore order if some members are getting out of hand, and generally other audience members will support you. You may also be expected to stop speakers from being unduly rude, vulgar, or offensive. A debate can and should be a lively event, but you should try to reduce any big barriers to rational consideration which arise from unseemly behavior.

Conducting a Vote. When the debate comes to a close, an audience vote may be expected. In keeping with the basic aim of public debate, this vote should indicate which side of the proposition the audience members support.

This is another time when you should give careful instructions to the audience about how the vote will be conducted. You can tell them that they are to vote for the position they agree with, not the best "team" of debaters. Tell them whether there will be a standing vote, a voice vote, or a written ballot. Some sets of rules, including parliamentary procedure, allow the audience to call for a "division" where votes are counted if the decision is close.

And if no formal vote is to be taken, you can suggest that they make up their minds individually. When there are actions they could take to implement their conclusions, such as voting on Tuesday or contacting their Congressmen, you can indicate these opportunities as well.

After the vote is counted, then you can announce how it came out and thank the audience for their attention. Finally you make any other necessary announcement, such as the date for the next debate. That's it.

As you can see, when you are in the chair you have a great deal of responsibility for making the debate a good one.

Chapter 5

Topics in the Public Realm

What's going on in the world? What are people thinking about? What do they really care about? The challenge and the enjoyment of discovering and selecting topics for public argument comes from being in the heart of the action. It keeps us alert to the world around us.

It gives us a bit of influence on the world around us, too. When we choose a topic for a public debate we are taking part in the creation of a public agenda as well. Deciding what topics to consider in our class or debating society constitutes our judgment about what is important, just like those of editors and other "agenda setters." Sometimes we will even select subjects not because everyone is talking about them, but because we think more people ought to be talking about them.

Let's say we have a debate on "Resolved, that real men don't eat quiche."

This topic, taken from the title of a popular and humorous book with a tongue-in-cheek wording allows an audience to explore the roles of men and women in society, especially when engaging teams from a coeducational and an all-male college, and opens up vital cultural value questions when taken beyond its narrow literal meaning.

"The Social Security trust fund will be broke by 2030."

When a question of presumable fact such as this one becomes a central concern for a public divided in its response to a current problem such as retirement income, it becomes a natural topic for speakers and audiences to investigate in a debating context.

"Resolved, that the Federal Government should significantly strengthen the regulation of mass media communication in the United States."

A carefully selected "national" college or high school topic, worded by a committee of experts and voted upon for its debatable qualities by forensics directors across the nation, a subject which will be thoroughly researched by hundreds of students throughout the country, can also be readily adapted to audience situations for a challenging and educational effect.

We can see that there is no shortage of topics for audience debate. You may have already looked at the list of subjects at the end of this chapter, and we have merely scratched the surface there with our suggestions. Perennial questions such as capital punishment and gun control have engaged popular attention for decades, while every daily newspaper report of an oil spill or crime spree creates a lively concern for the implied problems as well as new proposals for solving them.

Controversy is part of the air we breathe, and debates take place within the context of public concerns. We find good topics for debate by observing what the public is arguing about, and we select the ones to use by deciding where an exploration of the important issues can add the most to those arguments.

The selection of a suitable topic for an audience debate, as well as arriving at its best wording and clearest meaning, will be conducted with the attitudes and interests of prospective audiences as a fundamental concern.

All of the standard types of propositions may be suitable for public presentation. Any statement to which human assent may meaningfully be given will provide a basis for dispute, including propositions of policy, of value, of fact, and of definition.

Propositions of policy call for specific actions or policy alterations. They are readily grasped, are usually the focal point of debate in a decision-making democratic society, and students and other individuals are normally better trained to analyze policies than other types of proposals.

Propositions of value, probing the attitudes and preferences of the public, also make excellent topics, and the public debate platform sometimes makes an especially good place for such deliberation. Value judgments are arguably more dependent for confirmation upon public assent to them than are any other kind of proposition.

Even propositions of fact, such a hole in the ozone layer or a legal liability crisis, may be appropriate and controversial, especially where accumulated popular wisdom and judgment may have a bearing on the evaluation of sources of information and probabilities generally.

Finally, definitional propositions are not to be ignored, either. A community which has zoned out house trailers may very well become involved in a dispute as to whether modular homes, which come in on wheels but are placed on more permanent foundations, are included within the definition.

LOOKING FOR TOPICS

Prospective subjects for debate come at us from every direction. Mindful that our central motive is to contribute to meaningful deliberation about significant public issues and that direct personal involvement of the immediate participants is important in any debate, anyone planning such a debate or series of debates will follow a number of leads in locating and selecting the topics to be used.

Fundamental Issues. A public or private choice of a value or of a course of action may literally be a "life or death" matter. A choice between life and death, embodied in resolutions ranging from doctor-assisted suicide to nuclear proliferation, will be a fundamental one for any audience. An attention to what may be universal and pervasive will impel us to search for topics which focus on life and death, or upon equally engaging values as justice, freedom, virtue, and happiness.

Justice, freedom, virtue, and happiness may seem in our age too abstract for profitable debate, but a concentration upon these fundamental elements will help in the practical business of developing good debate topics. One asks, "What is really important, anyway?"' Where justice is at stake, for instance, the audience finds itself considering not only the immediate questions as to, say, the appropriate penalties for violent crime or resource distribution through the negative income tax, but also the more general matter of the nature of their society as a whole.

One can go back as far as Aristotle's *Rhetoric* to locate the ends of deliberative, forensic, and epideictic rhetoric. Even his specific listing of topics for political debate is timeless and universal enough to be useful as a guide to important topics today. His five-item list included ways and means, war and peace, national defense, imports and exports, and legislation.

No one has to go back to Aristotle, of course, to begin the search for a debate topic.

Timely Topics. While the universal and perennial issues are indeed significant, new subjects are constantly bubbling to the surface in the boiling kettle of public discourse. Every newspaper headline, every radio and television newscast, contains incipient controversial issues that energize public attention and speculation. Even the simple crime story, "Suspect in Triple Slaying Repudiates Confession," will suggest topics involving public order, jurisprudence, and police methods.

When newsworthy events stimulate discussion of the issues, alert scheduling of public debates has the advantage of "free advertising" as well as making a potential contribution to the discussion while it is the focus of public attention. In a class, some flexible time might well be left available for fast-breaking events. Some such events provoke renewed consideration of proposals and attitudes which have been neglected or were put on the back burner for a time. Other events, such as a successful case of in vitro fertilization or a spotted owl ruling, could bring more proposals or judgments into the public arena.

Rhetorical movements, through which groups of people attempt to create social change through public advocacy, may also provide issues through the controversy they generate. The women's rights movement, for example, focused serious public attention not only on the Equal Rights Amendment, but on divorce laws, property rights, day-care centers, wife abuse, rape crisis centers, and many others.

Direct Audience Concerns. Characterized by variations in social and economic status, age and sex, vocation, voluntary affiliations, and many other factors, the audiences themselves influence the selection of topics as they do almost every other element of public debate.

Audiences generate subjects. A demographic review of potential audiences will bring out propositions of interest to older people, to business leaders, to college students, to parents, and the like. The motives and interests of each group will provide the leads we need.

Even the specific locale may be important. Each community and each group has special controversies which emerge as unique to its situation. In a given town, the question of whether to erect a new stop light or a sewage disposal plant may be of considerable importance, though of no concern to the citizens of the next community. Indiana may be concerned about daylight saving time and Arizona the legalization of short-handled hoes. Audience debates are sometimes scheduled, particularly in the case of campus issues, for the specific purpose of assisting in the exploration of uniquely local issues of this kind.

Audience expertise is also an important element. Audiences consisting of college professors, engineers, accountants, recyclers, or even bicyclers provide knowledgeable participation in any debate related to their expertise, so we look for topics among the subjects which the audience members could be expected to know a lot about. Classes in school, of course, have debate topics built right into their syllabi. "Resolved, that Petrarch's ascent of Mount Ventoux marked the beginning of the Renaissance" might never be debated anywhere except in a college history class, but there it would certainly be appropriate enough.

As suggested earlier, invitations to debate for special audiences sometimes bring topics right along with them, as when the Indiana College Public Relations Association asked some students to come and debate the resolution that "Public relations is the blight on the ivy" as a program for their annual meeting.

The Participants. Persons who like to debate are usually interested in a good many different subjects. A "brainstorming" session among prospective participants in a debate or a series of debates will generate a number of potential topics about which these individuals are especially interested in speaking or upon which they happen to be well prepared and knowledgeable. In brainstorming for topics we consider the preferences and needs not only of the audience but also of the prospective principal speakers (such as the members of a debate team). You can schedule debates for the plain reason that there are individuals who have positions they want to advocate and debate publicly. You yourself may want to do that. Why not?

Creative Imagination. When audiences are given the necessary orientation, a wide range of more fanciful subjects may be debated. In parliamentary debating societies especially, the membership may want to argue on relatively unlikely subjects or on mind-stretchers which are not part of the day-to-day public deliberation. A British society enjoys debating that "'twould have been better had America never been discovered." A topic such as "Resolved, that logic is unreasonable" might be challenging.

Although not strictly in keeping with the rationale for public debating as we have described it, even humorous debates designed primarily for entertainment will sometimes be included in your schedule just for the fun of it.

Or DON'T be creative. Take a short cut and look at the list of sample topics in a book on public debating.

CHOOSING A TOPIC

All right, so there is no shortage of available topics for public debate. How do we decide whether to debate about international nuclear weapons control or about establishing the length of the school day in our community? How do we make that important decision? (Maybe we should settle it by debate.)

A large part of the answer is suggested by the sources of the propositions we have just surveyed. For instance, if we have hit upon a topic because it is timely and all the papers are talking about it, we make our decision to hold our public debate on that topic for the same reason: it is timely and all the papers are talking about it. As another example, if the audience for a particular debate (a business communication association chapter, say) has special interests, these interests will substantially influence our choice of a specific topic to debate there. And if a topic has been added to our list because it is interesting and vital to us personally as debaters, then we may choose to go public simply because we ourselves think the subject is important. The same forces which bring topics to our attention make them suitable for public debate.

When we look at the larger picture, we'll remember that one feature of audience debate is that it is supposed to make a difference. We're contributing to a significant public dialogue. That means that we will choose topics because they need to be debated. They're important. Members of the audience as members of the broader society are trying to discover arguments for and against the proposition in order to make up their minds as rationally as possible. We therefore select for debate matters which people are worried about and whose potential resolution will perform a service for our community as well.

Another criterion for us to meet in the selection of a proposition for a particular debate is the extent to which these audience members are likely to get involved in the subject. Since one of the things we are looking for is active participation by a large number of people, the topic should be one which relates to their basic needs and concerns, or touches upon fundamental values which may be in conflict among a set of audience members. Thus even a rather narrow topic such as whether motorcycle riders should be required to wear helmets may tap reservoirs of feelings about risk-taking, masculinity, government controls, and the like. In addition, for purposes of involvement, the topic should normally be one which the audience is sufficiently informed about to feel comfortable in expressing their opinions in open debate, and where they can apply their knowledge, their experience, and their stock of values.

We do, therefore, want to ask the further question whether the audience knows enough to take part in a debate on this topic. Some cynics will say that the public is too ignorant to debate about much of anything meaningfully. We're not enthusiastic about that assertion. In any event, public debate has an educational function and provides one method for making people less ignorant. Still, a reasonably knowledgeable audience probably makes for a more profitable debate, and propositions may sometimes be selected with that observation in mind.

Capital punishment and gun control have been mentioned as examples of "perennial" questions. Such topics are worth paying attention to because they have continued to be matters of controversy for a long time. They must tap a nerve. In fact, if you are planning your first public debate, we would recommend one of these topics. A debate on the topic, "Resolved, that private ownership of hand guns should be prohibited by law," gets you into such fundamental matters as the relationship of the individual and government, Constitutional interpretations, pragmatic threats and dangers, and even relatively subliminal issues such as the value and definition of "manliness." Furthermore, we might add, most people know enough and have clear enough opinions to participate comfortably in such a debate. And it's bound to be lively.

Naturally, we may not be limited to choosing a topic for just one debate. We hope to have more. When we are in an argumentation class or a debating society, or we're sponsoring a series of debates, a further consideration in topic selection will be "building" the audience qualitatively and perhaps quantitatively. With practice, as audience members get better at analysis as well as the discovery and use of evidence, they can profitably handle more complex subjects and may be led to work on propositions of different kinds and in different fields. They may never have dealt with a controversy about a presumable scientific fact, so the time may be ripe to try one. As a series of debates continues, variety and complexity may become standards for selection of topics. We're asking, "What would be good for these people to debate right now?"

There may be things not to debate, too. Speaking of humor, for instance, we will suggest going slowly on the utilization of facetious topics. Some speakers and even some organizations are attracted to such propositions as "Worms are more disgusting than spiders" because they might be easy and funny. However, humor without a substantive base is remarkably difficult to sustain, especially if you are not practiced in it. The previously mentioned proposition about quiche is saved only by the fact that it implies some serious arguments. Save absurd topics for special occasions when you know that's what people are looking for.

One other type of subject not to debate too much is the completely one-sided topic (as gauged by the audience, of course). Sometimes persons are eager to hear debates or to participate in them because they are strongly in favor of the proposal, or even emotionally attracted to it, forgetting that perhaps everyone else who is likely to attend is also strongly committed to the same position. The ensuing situation of one or two persons holding off the masses may be dramatic, but it does not necessarily produce a good public debate event.

WORDING THE PROPOSITION

Now to formulate an exact wording for the topic you have selected. Even the way we word the topic for debate will depend a great deal upon the needs and expectations of the prospective audience. We won't stop here to give examples of horrendously bad propositions or ideally perfect ones, but you can peruse the list at the end of this chapter and practice applying some of the guidelines for wording which we suggest here.

For openers, any debate proposition should be stated as clearly and fairly as possible. Clarity and fairness are the time-tested standards for formulating propositions, demanded both by logical requirements and the necessities of audience participation. Clarity requires that the most precise words and phrases be used and that ambiguities be avoided. Fairness requires that the proposition not be stated in a one-sided manner and that "loaded language" be avoided. We'll remember, of course, that all language is abstract and value-laden, so we can never achieve that perfect wording, but applying the standards of clarity and fairness to the best of our abilities should give us better argumentation. Do the best you can and get on with the debate.

In public debating there may well be a difference between the wording of a proposition as it is announced for publicity purposes and a more precise "actual" formulation. For posters and announcements, for instance, shortened versions are frequently employed, such as when the topic "Resolved, that the private possession of hand guns should be prohibited," mentioned earlier, is debated. For these purposes, the topic may even appear as a phrase ("Gun control") or as a question ("Should hand guns be outlawed?") in order to make it easy to grasp. Words may also be selected for their stylistic attention-getting or retention qualities, such as a publicly announced campus proposition that "Coeducation is no education." Or they may be designed simply to be provocative, such as "A liberal arts diploma is not worth the paper it is printed on," where a literal interpretation would not be expected by the audience. A specific event as an example may be referred to in the public wording, particularly if it involves a contemporary or newsworthy reference.

No matter how carefully the proposition may have been worded, speakers may disagree about what it means.   However, public argument about semantics or "topicality" is not usually very productive. No debate can go forward without agreement about what is actually being debated.   Therefore, in cases of doubt we recommend that the advocates reach an agreement among themselves before the debate takes place in order to settle possible points of confusion or doubt. That agreement may be formulated in a proposition which is more meticulously worded than the one which has been announced on the posters, and the full statement may be set forth explicitly by the chair or the opening speaker at the beginning of the debate. Sometimes reaching agreement concerning the formal wording calls for relatively careful negotiations between representatives of the two sides. A pre-debate agreement of this kind may also include a certain stipulation or parameter which goes beyond the statement of the proposition. In one debate, where the affirmative was advocating that an International Environmental Protection Treaty be ratified, a time factor was negotiated in which it was agreed that the treaty must be ratified within five years, and not just "eventually."

Ultimately, what a proposition means is what the audience thinks it means. Even stipulated understandings may be rejected if they too greatly violate audience interpretations and expectations. In a debate that's supposed to be about a "national health care system," if the meaning of that phrase is so attenuated, even by agreement among the principal speakers, that the listeners cannot identify it as such, then the listeners can and will speak and debate according to interpretations which make more sense to them. Trick cases do not belong in public debate. Again, the judgment about what constitute undue liberties with terminology belongs to the voting audience. Teams who are advocating conservation of scarce resources and claim that "money" is a scarce resource will gain acceptance only from listeners who have left their brains in the hall closet. Some care, it should be noted, will often be necessary in using the "national" high school or college topics, where a good deal of leeway in interpretation has been established as a tournament norm. The best practice in wording is to reveal explicitly what will be debated, so that if advocates of greater regulation of land use are planning to limit their arguments to the aspect of transportation, then just announce in the first place that the debate is going to be about transportation.

Propositions should be worded as single declarative sentences which may be affirmed or denied. This being said, we should realize that topics subject to public debate are almost always more complex than anything which can be boiled down to a single sentence. In debating propositions of policy, for instance, most advocates will set forth a "plan" which explains in much greater detail the nature of the proposal which serves as the basis of argument. Some debates call for consideration of a whole law which is to be voted upon by a legislative body, so although the resolution might simply call for approval of, say, an Omnibus Crime Bill, the debate would be about the whole complex of variegated provisions contained in that bill. In another instance, a debate on a value proposition such as "Resolved, that small is beautiful" might well call for approval or disapproval of a whole relatively sophisticated position set forth in a book by that title.

And sometimes one finds it difficult to avoid wording a proposition in question form, which is a logical no-no. When public discourse has reached a point where one of two mutually exclusive proposals is to be adopted, a declarative wording tends to give the advantage to one side or the other. In such a case, it is better to put the either/or controversy into question form, such as, "Should the new stadium be built in the present location or in a suburban area?" Political debates are perfect examples of this situation, where one side wants to prove that Candidate A should be elected and the other side favors Candidate B. Furthermore, those unusual topics which require three sides to be represented (or even 8 sides, as in an 8-sided political primary debate) also suggest the utilization of a question form for the formal proposition.

PRESUMPTION AND BURDEN OF PROOF

You have frequently heard the term "burden of proof," no doubt. The burden of proof is a traditional argumentation concept which designates the "burden" which one side or the other is supposed to carry. They are required to meet certain proof requirements in order to gain rational assent or their position will be summarily rejected.

A "presumption" then rests with the side which does not carry this burden, the party who would be just as satisfied if the debate were never held. In criminal law there is an arbitrary "presumption of innocence," for instance. A person is presumed innocent until the prosecution meets its burden of proof, to demonstrate guilt beyond a reasonable doubt. In some debate theories you would find that presumption in policy questions is assigned to the status quo. The burden is placed upon the advocate who wants to change that status quo.

In much public debate the concept of burden of proof is not so useful. The location of the burden of proof, like most other aspects, depends upon audience attitudes, so it will change from audience to audience and, indeed, will vary from one listener to another. Who has the burden when half the audience is for the negative at the beginning of a debate, but the other half is for the affirmative?

There is a traditional rule in debate that the proposition should be worded so that the affirmative side carries the burden of proof. This is why the affirmative side is frequently allowed to give not only the first speech in the debate, but the last one as well (as you may have noticed in Chapter 3). However, you may not even know ahead of time which side the audience favors and therefore who would be unhappy if the debate didn't take place. About the best we can do in wording the proposition is to make an informed guess as to which side is likely to have the toughest row to hoe and give them the affirmative.

In Chapter 6, as you try to answer the question, "What does it take to prove this proposition?", you may want to consider whether the side you are defending has a psychological or assigned presumption or burden of proof in a given debate. This may help you to decide what contentions to stress. No one in a public debate can really afford to assert too complacently, however, that "I'm right until you prove me wrong." You always should be prepared to support whatever you assert in a debate.

As a basic rule, propositions should be chosen and worded in ways which will best facilitate rational public deliberation and decision making.

SOME TESTED DEBATE PROPOSITIONS

Note: The following sample propositions are largely stock matters of public controversy, and all have been used successfully by students engaging in public debate.

Capital punishment should be abolished throughout the United States

A balanced budget amendment should be added to the United States Constitution

The United States should adopt a system of universal health care

Prayer should be permitted in the public schools

Doctor-assisted suicide should be legalized for terminally ill patients

The institution of school voucher systems would be desirable

The Supreme Court's Roe v. Wade decision should be reversed

The possession of marijuana should be decriminalized

Women should be allowed to hold combat positions in the military

The drinking age should be lowered to 18 throughout the nation

This institution should adopt an honor code

Note: The following propositions have in recent years been selected by the Cross Examination Debate Association for nationwide intercollegiate debate. They have all proven usable in public debates.

Resolved, that increased restrictions on the civilian possession of handguns would be justified

Resolved, that violence is a justified response to political oppression

Resolved, that government censorship of public artistic expression in the United States is an undesirable infringement on individual rights

Resolved, that U.S. colleges and universities have inappropriately altered educational practices to address issues of race or gender

Resolved, that advertising degrades the quality of life in the United States

Resolved, that the welfare system exacerbates the problems of the urban poor in the United States

Resolved, that the United Nations implementation of its Universal Declaration of Human Rights is more important than preserving state sovereignty

Resolved, that the national news media in the United States impair the public's understanding of political issues

Resolved, that United States military intervention to foster democratic government is appropriate in a post-Cold War world

Chapter 6

Analysis of Propositions and Audiences

Now that you have chosen a proposition and worded it as carefully as you can, you will begin to look at it more systematically in order to prepare for the actual debate.

The chances are that you already have a pretty good idea of what the controversy is all about. If you have been at all involved in the process of deciding what topic you are going to use and how you're going to word it for a particular debate, then you have become aware of the argument swirling around it and a lot of the pros and cons about it. You know some of the reasons people usually present when they are arguing about this subject.

At this point, then, after your proposition has been decided upon, you begin to analyze it more systematically and break it down into manageable parts. This process of breaking down or dividing a proposition into parts is called analysis. You have to figure out what it takes to prove (or disprove) the proposition for the audience you'll be facing.

The "parts" which you are trying to discover in analyzing a proposition in argumentation and debate are called issues. Locating issues will help you to choose the important reasons for supporting (or rejecting) the proposition and eventually to select what you want to say to your audience.

What exactly are issues? Issues are questions which set the basic ground for pro and con argument about the proposition. Note that they are usually questions and not declarative statements. Normally they are worded so that they can be answered "yes" or "no" (preferably "yes" be the affirmative side) and they tell you where the major points of clash are potentially going to be.

An example of an issue which could come up in many different debates might be, "Can we afford to pay for the proposed plan?" An affirmative would answer "yes" to this question and the negative would quite possibly say "no." When the debate takes place, though, we won't have to be too disturbed if the issue is for rhetorical purposes worded negatively ("Will the plan cost too much?") or not as a yes-or-no question ("How can we pay for it?"). We still have a major issue.

Some of the questions you isolate may be regarded as sub-issues, which are issues which need to be resolved in the course of settling a major issue. And other questions may be classified as minor issues, which stand relatively independent of other issues but are not necessarily regarded as important enough to be decisive in themselves.

Because you will be engaged in a public activity where others are also debating on the subject, and because you may assume a certain amount of rationality on the part of those who are engaged in this public dialogue, the primary place you will want to look for the issues which are likely to be central to your own debate is among the available discourse on the subject. In other words, you can read up on the topic and can talk about it with other people. As you find the people who are engaged in this controversy stressing one point or another, you can begin to focus your note taking on these points and subpoints.

The process, then, is primarily one of searching and sorting. If, for instance, you are going to debate a proposal that the United States should resume the production of chemical warfare gasses, you may find proponents saying such things as that a problem exists due to the deterioration of present stockpiles of such gasses, or that the United States must have such gasses in production to meet a presumed foreign threat of the use of such weapons or to provide a deterrent to their use by other nations. Other advocates will oppose the proposal and say such things as that it would seriously undermine our moral position against the use of such weapons and give the other nations an excuse to go ahead with their own production and, furthermore, that the proposal would be unacceptable to allies in Europe where the nerve gasses might be used. You would also find people talking about the apparent current use of gas in certain conflicts in Southeast Asia or the Middle East, while other advocates are concerned with problems of verifiability in arms control agreements.

A major issue in the chemical warfare debate might turn out to be, "Will the production of binary chemical nerve gas weapons strengthen the strategic position of the United States?" The affirmative says yes and the negative says no, and both sides give a substantial amount of attention to this question.

Analysis of the ongoing controversy should include a serious consideration of both the history of the topic and the immediate cause for discussion of it.

Examine, for one thing, the history of the question. Those issues which have persisted over the years may be regarded as significant ones. Take a look at articles and books written twenty or thirty (or 120!) years ago and see what familiar themes are present. Those matters which are recurrent are frequently central to the proposition and will be so regarded by the members of your audience.

Look also at the immediate cause for discussion and the current status of the question. New events may have transpired, bringing the topic to the fore in the public mind. Or a fresh proposal may have been made which calls for the rearranging of the reasons for and against the proposition. In the case of gas warfare, for instance, the proposal for production and storage of a "binary" gas, having two parts neither of which is fatal in itself, calls for modification of storage arguments and a fresh issue concerning whether the new proposal overcomes reservations about such storage. Reports of use of nerve gas in remote parts of the world also call for a renewed look at the issue of whether anyone would dare to use such gasses.

Your first and most important resource in the analysis of the proposition you are going to debate is the examination of what people are saying about it. It is in the ongoing total public debate that the issues are best to be seen.

STOCK ANALYSIS

However, investigation of the on-going controversy is not the only available procedure for discovering the issues in your proposition. You may, if you wish, look at the proposition itself and try to analyze it logically without reference to what anyone else may be saying.

Some people think that's the best way to do it. Logical theorists have put a good deal of effort into trying to figure out what it takes to prove a proposition. Much of this theory ignores the audiences and assumes that what is logical for one person will be just as logical for another.

Analyzing the proposition in this rather traditional way may be advantageous to you in several ways. (1) It will supplement what you have already done and perhaps give you some ideas you hadn't thought of. (2) The analytical demands which have seemed reasonable to generations of scholars will probably give you some clues as to the likely demands of your audience. Thus it is worth your while to proceed with this relatively detached intellectual analysis as you prepare for your debate.

The easiest approach to traditional analysis is through the "stock issues" approach. It has been contended that there are certain issues which are vital in argumentation, especially on propositions of policy, no matter what the specific proposition is. These issues can be used in debate on just about any proposition you happen to choose.

Policy Propositions. Most textbook attention has been given to methods for analyzing propositions of policy, the kind which call for implementation of some proposed action and which are, of course, commonly in dispute in the public forum. Any advocates should be familiar with the various procedures which have been developed for discovering issues in propositions of policy as they have been elaborated in texts, professional journals, and papers.

For instance, the best established approach to a stock analysis of a policy proposition is called a "needs" approach, so you should get to know the kinds of questions it raises. These questions may be raised with respect to almost any policy proposal.

1. Is there a problem, a need for a change?
2. Does the proposal or plan meet the need and solve the problem?
3. Is the plan practical for implementation?
4. Do the advantages outweigh the disadvantages?

As you can see, these questions meet our criteria for "issues" quite well.

Fully to examine such stock issues also requires attention to important sub-issues, most notably harms (is the problem set forth genuinely harmful?), significance (are these harms of consequential extent quantitatively and qualitatively?), and inherency (is the problem so much a part of the status quo that it cannot be solved without a fundamental change of the sort which is proposed?)

A somewhat different stock analytical approach to propositions of policy, with which students who have been engaged in tournament debating will be especially familiar, is called the "comparative advantages" analysis. In this approach, the main point is not so much what is wrong with the status quo as the advantages which would accrue from some change in it. The stock issues which emerge from a comparative advantages approach typically include:

1. Is this plan feasible?
2. Will the asserted advantages accrue?
3. Do the advantages outweigh the disadvantages?

Harm, significance, and inherency may likewise play a part in this form of analysis.

In asking what has to be proved in order to prove a proposition of policy, affirmative and negative debaters will normally apply such stock methods of analysis along with the rest of their preparation.

Value Propositions. Less explicit guidance is available in traditional debate books regarding analysis of a second type of proposition, the proposition of value. A value proposition does not call directly for action, but for approval or disapproval with respect to some moral standard or aesthetic criterion. Examples of such propositions given in Chapter 5 included "Resolved, that meeting energy needs is more important than preserving the environment" and "Violence is a justified response to politcal oppression."

To conduct an objective analysis of essentially subjective judgments has always posed difficulties in argumentation theory.

The most common stock method for locating issues in value controversies is to define the key value term in the proposition. Once you know what you mean by "more important" or "basic human right," you can derive issues from that meaning. Thus the issues in a proposition using the terminology "more important" as a key term might appear in this form:

1. Does the value affect more persons?
2. Does it affect them in fundamental ways?
3. Does it avoid conflict with other values?

Thus the formulation of the definition becomes a basis for what must be proven in the debate.

Other approaches to the analysis of value propositions would include (1) the establishment of a hierarchy of values in which the values supported or rejected in the resolution are compared within a structure of higher and lower values, (2) a standard of consistency in which issues are derived from the consonance of the supporting arguments themselves, and (3) a method of consequences in which the values are judged in terms of the actions which they sanction or imply.

Other forms of propositions, such as the proposition of fact, have been subjected to even less theoretical scrutiny in argumentation theory, but in these the issues also tend to be derived from definition and from the application of empirical observation.

Whatever the proposition under consideration, one may look at the subject matter and the particular wording to see what the potential logical demands are for the establishment of its proof and to see what issues are thereby suggested.

AUDIENCE ANALYSIS

There is yet a third locale for you to explore in your search for potential issues. In audience debating, all standards ultimately exist in the minds of your audience members, so you now have to figure out whether there are some concerns of the audience which are so important that they may create issues. A question may be an issue for one particular audience and yet be of no concern at all to another.

For instance, an issue formulated as "Will this proposal be of benefit to farmers?" may be of overwhelming concern to an audience in a rural area and of relatively little moment to urban listeners.

Demographic Analysis. A demographic analysis of your audience would consist of a survey of the general characteristics of its members. You might look at such factors as the following:

1. Age
2. Sex
3. Economic status
4. Education
5. Locale
6. Race
7. Occupation
8. Affiliations

Using a list such as this permits you to see whether there may be potential issues. Most of them you would probably ignore in any given debate, but as with the issue of the farmers, the locale or occupation could be quite significant and should not be overlooked.

In the proposition concerning resumption of production of chemical warfare gasses, the residents of central Kentucky might be very much concerned about the issue of "Can a safe storage place be located?" because central Kentucky is one of the places where such gasses are stored.

An audience which is made up of quite young people might have different concerns and even different attitudes from an elderly audience. These concerns could range from specific matters of self-interest on such topics as social security or the military draft to general attitudes about whether change is desirable in itself. Traditional guidelines concerning the conservatism of age or the radicalism of youth must be used with some discretion, of course, as there are such things as conservative youths and radical old people.

Attitudes and Values. Audiences at a certain time and place may also have attitudes and values which are not directly related to their demographic characteristics, and these attitudes and values may be fundamental enough to generate potential issues.

For instance, individuals who have a strong consciousness of a Soviet threat to the United States may have as an uppermost concern an issue such as "Will this proposal strengthen the United States vis a vis the Russians?" Another audience may be extremely concerned about the preservation of the traditional family, and where this is relevant to a given proposition will respond to the issues of "Does this proposal preserve the family?"

An audience may be made up largely of persons who have a humane concern about the welfare of those less fortunate in society, so "Does this proposal help those less fortunate?" emerges as an issue in debates before such an audience.

The Specific Audience. Any specific audience before whom you are going to debate may well have specific characteristics of its own.

They may, for instance, be members of a certain special interest organization or club. They may be majors in a certain subject in school.

If you are quite familiar with the audience and have observed or participated in debates with that audience before, you may have noticed their more or less habitual response to certain kinds of issues. They may have, for instance, in previous debates responded to a "no harm done" argument. An issue which might emerge in a debate with such an audience is "Can the proposal be implemented with little risk?" You will no doubt be especially familiar with such matters if you are a member of a class, a club, or a debating society which meets and debates regularly.

Remember that what you are generating from your audience analysis is potential issues which you should research and be prepared to debate about. Which ones will turn out to be vital in the long run will eventually be determined in the process of the debate itself.

CENTRALITY

When they are analyzing propositions, debaters try not only to achieve thoroughness in the discovery of all of the potential issues they can find, but they also make choices about which issue is most important. They know that in a debate they will have to focus on some aspect of the question, not infrequently on just one aspect, in order to make their position meaningful and manageable.

Although the central focus of the controversy will emerge during the course of the debate itself, your preliminary analysis should no doubt include a development of a position concerning where that focus should be.

One reason why centrality is important in audience debate is that normally a good many persons contribute their ideas before the debate is over, so that a focus on some central idea gives you a chance to sort out the disparate ideas presented and perhaps demonstrate connecting threads among them. A second reason for attending to centrality is that any given debate inherently has time constraints which keep you from covering everything, so you have to be selective.

Here we are going to suggest that in analyzing your proposition and preparing for your debate you give some thought to centrality in three regards: (1) the central issue, (2) a central value, and (3) a central drama. Obviously, the matter loses some of its centrality if these three items are too removed from one another, so the central issue, central value, and central drama should normally reflect the same basic thrust in your argument.

Central Issue. Issues are formulated on the basis of rigorous and thorough analysis of what the proposition is all about. In the course of such analysis, some potential issues are eventually minimized because they are of subordinate importance and others are set aside because they are one-sided and not a matter of real dispute. Advocates who are attempting to set forth the most reasonable and effective arguments in support of their positions will normally attempt to find one issue which stands out.

Frequently, for instance, an affirmative side will see the problem area as central and will declare that the central issue is "Does a significant problem exist?" They may figure that once this issue is decided, namely that a problem such as acid rain, a flood of imports, or a subversive threat in Central America exists and is significant, the rest of the matters under dispute will fall into place quite naturally.

On the other hand, the negative position on a proposition may turn out to rest substantially on the issue of practicality, "Can the proposal be enforced?" They may want to settle whether proposals with regard to seat belts, drinking age laws, or nuclear arms agreements are practical enough to be seriously considered. Other issues may be regarded as subordinate to these.

All of the advocates in the debate, including the audience members who speak, can ask themselves what the central issue is and how determining it should be in the final decision-making.

Central Value. Analysis may also well reveal that one central value stands out as most important for deliberation, even when the proposition is one concerned with policy. Public debate is inherently a matter of determining preferences, and preferences rest ultimately upon the values which audience members have.

You might decide in the course of your analysis, for instance, that the dispute you are working on boils down to a matter of "freedom of choice." You would reinforce the importance of that value with the audience and reformulate an issue to ask, "Does this proposal reinforce freedom of choice?" In another instance, with a different proposition or a different audience, the central value around which other values and arguments would cluster might be "self preservation." Keep your mind alert to the values which are implied within the proposition you are analyzing.

Keep in mind that the process of locating the central value position is one which rests upon knowing your audience as well as knowing your subject. The value you choose must be one which your listeners will respond to in order for it to be used as a focal point of speeches during the debate.

Central Drama. A debate is also a drama. No matter what the topic is, the controversy has a strong dramatic element including such features as characters, plots, and scenes. Audience identification and involvement are most often achieved as the listeners become wrapped up in the ongoing suspense and the conflict inherent in the debate situation.

There is, then, a strong dramatic conflict in the immediate debate event itself. Two sides are in conflict and these sides are represented by living, talking characters in a structured scenario calling for audience response. Arguments may be selected and presented with this important context in mind.

But also, the subject area of the proposition being debated is normally filled with dramatic possibilities. All the world's a stage. The utilization of plot structures such as solving a problem, overcoming an obstacle, or conflicts between good and evil are important elements in your analysis. Likewise, since arguments are populated by people, the characters of the drama will be located, identified, and made real to the audience.

The establishment of scene, plot, and character is as vital as any other part of the argument for representing the strongest possible position on a proposition, and thus the drama being played forth by each side may itself be a matter of legitimate clash. An advocate favoring a program of national health care, for example, may dramatize cases of persons, or "characters," whose lives are wrecked by inordinate medical expenses. Opponents may dramatize the struggle of doctors and dentists to achieve their competence and the threat from a nationalization policy to the rewards they have earned. And the audience, of course, will have to decide where their sympathies reside and which characters they identify with the most.

Sometimes a single paradigmic example, such as Sam Sheppard in the case of a proposition having to do with press freedom or Bernhard Goetz in the case of vigilantism, may be familiar to your audience and can provide easy access to the dramatic element of your debate.

Keep in mind, as you search out the central drama in your proposition, that this drama will have the most effect argumentatively if it is strikingly coordinated with the central issue and the central value which you are planning to stress in the debate. As the members of your audience set the arguments they hear within a dramatic framework they more easily respond to and evaluate the contentions being set forth.

CASE CONSTRUCTION

So far you have been taking an overview of the whole proposition as you have analyzed its potential issues, but there comes a time when you have to start selecting the contentions you will be using in a particular debate. If you are one of the principal speakers, or if you have a deep commitment to one side of the question, then you will prepare the "case" which you will present in defending or opposing it.

A case consists of your interpretation of the proposition and your rationale for its acceptance or rejection. You can think of it as an organized speech which you might give. As a first speaker in a debate you will be expected to have a prepared speech, and each of the other speakers may well have prepared some "constructive" material to be presented.

The investigation which you have been doing as you analyzed the proposition has probably revealed to you some of the stronger and more appropriate lines of argument on your side (and the other side).

So far you have been formulating the issues, and therefore you have a set of basic questions to consider. In constructing a case, you now transform the questions into contentions. For instance, an issue which you can see as important may have been worded, "Is acid rain a serious problem?" To word this issue as a contention for the affirmative side, you might end up with something like,

"Acid rain is a serious problem."

Forming a case means deciding what specific contentions you are going to defend and establishing supports for those contentions. Now, for instance, you would be thinking about support for the contention that "Acid rain is a serious problem." Your previous research has already suggested a number of reasons why this is so. You then proceed as in organizing a speech to select subcontentions which would be effective for the audience you will be addressing. An example might be,

"Acid rain is harmful to forest resources."

You would look for evidence that this was so and add that evidence to your case. What you end up with is an outline of a speech reflecting a coherent set of arguments for your side.

The negative side, as well as the affirmative, prepares its case before the debate. For some issues, this means preparing responses to what the affirmative is likely to say. You might prepare ahead of time to support the contention that "Acid rain is not a serious problem." You might also have constructive arguments that serve to diminish the strength of affirmative cases no matter what case the affirmative chooses to present. Such a contention might be, for example, that "The proposal is morally unjustifiable."

Part of your speech will be an explanation of what the proposal means to you. Especially if you are debating about a proposition of policy, you will need to construct a "plan" showing exactly what actions you are calling for. In a proposition of value, this explication will give a fuller view of the proposition. These elements will no doubt constitute part of the constructive materials you include in your presentation.

Your "case," then, will in effect be an outline of a speech for or against the proposition, and it will be based upon a general position and will include your explanation of the meaning of the proposition and a well-chosen and well-supported set of contentions on your side.

Throughout your preparation of your case try to keep uppermost in your mind the analytical consideration, "What are the central issues upon which a decision will hinge in this debate?"

EMERGENT ANALYSIS

As you have seen, the issues in a debate are points of fundamental clash on a given proposition. Thus they are dependent upon what advocates for the opposing positions choose to say, since these questions don't become issues if no one talks about them.

What you have been accumulating so far is a set of potential issues which seem to be governing the controversy. A good many of the potential issues which have been derived from the investigation you have conducted, such as from stock issues or from current public discourse, will have converged. That is, some of the issues come up over and over again no matter how you analyze the topic. Others show up only from a single point of view.

The potential issues you have formulated are useful in your preparation because they provide a basis for selection and anticipation of contentions to be used in the debate.

You will not know the actual issues, of course, until the debate takes place. One of several things may happen. One of them is that the issues which you have decided are important turn out to be the same ones which your opponents and the audience think are important, and these points easily emerge as the real issues.

Another thing which may happen is that some of the issues you have selected to talk about become actual issues, while others fade out of the debate because the matters involved are admitted or agreed to by the two sides or because they are dismissed as of no particular interest to anyone.

A third thing which can happen is that new issues may come out of the clash of opinions in the debate you are in. Sometimes a point which you did not think was important will become a focal point because of the development of the clash in the debate. For instance, the reliability of a particular authority may rise to the status of an issue if one side relies heavily upon that "expert" and the other side insists that the person is a nerd.

A final way in which issues may emerge in the debate you are conducting takes the form of a clash over whether or not a given question is indeed an issue at all. One side thinks that it is and the other side thinks that it isn't. Thus the question of whether the matter should be regarded as an issue itself becomes an issue.

Throughout the debate a continuing analysis should be taking place, with advocates on both sides periodically making explicit their perceptions of "These are the issues in this debate."

Chapter 7

Premises in Public Debate

One of the paradoxes of debate is that in order to have argumentation, you must have a substantial amount of agreement to begin with. If two individuals agree about everything, they don't need to debate; if they disagree about everything, they can't debate. Among the basic ingredients of a debate are the "premises" which are acceptable enough to the decision-makers to serve as a basis for constructing an argument.

Premises are statements to which listeners will readily grant their assent and which may be used in combination to generate adherence to further conclusions. Perelman refers to them as "the starting points of argument."

After we have done some preliminary analysis, one of our first tasks as public debaters is to search out usable premises. Research is an investigation of subject matter with the audience in mind. The wide variety of premises we'll be looking for includes known information audience members are likely to have, fresh information, expert opinions, values to which they may subscribe, and characteristic patterns of reasoning.

For instance, if debaters are defending a Proposition 13 type of resolution calling for automatic reduction of taxation via some established formula, they could look for premises of the following kinds:

The degree to which listeners are acquainted with public budgets, rates of taxation, bureaucratic procedures, and past results of legislation of this type.

Fresh information, revealed through standard research methods, which the audience cannot be expected to be familiar with, but which will be regarded as probable and acceptable to them.

Expert opinions from sources which will be regarded as credible by listeners.

Values that listeners are likely to hold as represented in their attitudes toward government, toward taxation, toward special services, toward individual responsibility, and the like.

Field dependent and general rules of thinking which can serve as warrants in the reasoning process.

If any premise is challenged in a debate, of course, it becomes a matter of dispute and thus as controvertible as anything else. What debaters are looking for are premises which are well established and can withstand rigorous challenge and scrutiny.

Naturally, the available premises one accumulates must be relevant to the proposition under consideration. This fact suggests that research and analysis are reciprocal processes. The potential issues which you have discovered in your analysis will lead you to look for evidence which relates to them. And as you examine the evidence, new issues may emerge as well. Even during a debate you may find yourself using information in ways you had not anticipated and motivated to look for fresh information on a matter you had not considered important or relevant before.

WHAT THEY ALREADY KNOW AND BELIEVE

Since a premise is a statement to which the audience adheres, we will probably want to find out what our listeners already know and believe about the subject. This means engaging in a continuation of the audience analysis which was an important part of our previous analysis of the proposition.

In this further analysis of the audience, as was suggested above, we can look for usable premises in their previous experience and knowledge, in the values to which they subscribe, in their likely frames of reference or world view, in the patterns of thinking they tend to employ, and in the sources they trust.

What They Know. Anything a person has experienced or observed personally is bound to make an impression of some kind. If your listeners have been in an automobile accident or have seen the condition of the city parks or have been caught in what they regard as bureaucratic red tape, you will be able to build conclusions from such experiences.

You may try to make yourself aware of the experiences of the particular group you are talking with. A business group will know about a recent bankruptcy in the community; a parents' group will be familiar with their local textbooks. Even the experience of the immediate occasion provides us with useful evidence. In one debate speakers and listeners manifestly preened themselves and faked attention as a news photographer crept about the room, thus providing first-hand disconfirmation for an important contention that cameras would have little effect in courtroom situations.

Of course, what the members of any audience know goes far beyond their own personal experience. Most listeners you will address are immersed in an information society. They know about the Alaskan oil spill; they are familiar with the Constitutional Bill of Rights; they have followed various hostage crises. There is a vast store of "common knowledge" upon which you can normally draw in selecting premises for your argumentation. Some recent commentary has shed doubt on how vast this store of common knowledge actually is, but even when you do not know much about your specific audience you can make assumptions based upon this common knowledge.

The premises you formulate do not have to be limited to the empirical tidbits often referred to as "facts," either. Much of what we know is bundled into more generalized truths. We may assert that "extremes of wealth and poverty exist on this planet" as a premise without citing specific examples. An audience may well accept the idea that "space exploration is a risky business" or that "educated persons make more money." Even general folk wisdom, often expressed in aphorisms such as "you can't teach an old dog new tricks" or "you get what you pay for," may provide acceptable premises within a debate context.

In planning your arguments, then, you start with a keen eye upon what the audience apparently already knows and believes.

Their Values. Beyond the information which listeners possess, they subscribe to values which guide them in making judgments about propositions they are asked to consider.

Values are personal and social preferences concerning what is right or wrong, good or evil, beautiful or ugly. "Life" and "liberty," for instance, are two values to which most members of the American culture would subscribe. These values are available for use as accepted premises in debates before many audiences. Some other value, such as, say, "enjoy yourself," might be subscribed to strongly by one audience and rejected by another. So once more, analysis of your audience is necessary to discover available premises.

The values individuals hold usually structure themselves either into hierarchies or into polar opposites. In a hierarchical structure, some values are seen as more important than others. Some persons might value the taste of chocolate and also value their family ties. They might really like some chocolate, but would be willing to give it up to maintain harmony in the family (if that should become necessary). Members of a community may prefer "low taxes," but will be willing to vote for a new school building if "education of our children" is an even higher value.

When values are looked at in polar terms, you can try to determine where listeners stand on them. Some audiences may lean heavily in the direction of "cooperation" as a desirable goal; others may see "competition" as uppermost. The audience will judge an argument to be acceptable when it is based upon the values to which they most strongly adhere.

And values themselves, no matter how deeply held, are themselves debatable. We may have to argue for certain values before we can use them as premises. In any event, one important source of premises is going to be the values held by the individuals in the audience.

Their World View. With varying degrees of explicitness, the individuals who compose public audiences possess world views or frames of reference which also guide their reasoning. They have different ways of looking at what the world is like and how it operates.

For instance, some may see the world as a vast arena for the struggle of good vs. evil, where most of their experiences and motives line up in one or the other camp. That's one frame of reference. Others may look at their world through the spectacles of whole religious, economic, or political systems or theories. We live in a God-governed universe for some, while for others everything may seem to be determined economically. Some see reality as essentially predetermined; others subscribe to free-will assumptions.

Whether you are going to use as a premise a relatively fatalistic view ("if it happens, it happens") or a purposive one ("you can make a difference") will depend to some extent upon whatever view of their world the audience members seem to have.

Patterns of Thought. Some of the premises which you will need to have available are formulations of the way audience members think. For example, if you are debating gun control, you may want to use an analogy like "What is true of England is true of the United States." Most but not all individuals will at least entertain an analogy when used as a premise.

Some patterns of thought are regarded as universal in application. When you use a deduction from general to specific ("What is true of all lesser developed nations is probably true of Zaire") or induction from the specific to the general ("What is true in Zaire is likely to be true in all LDNs"), you are using patterns which are widespread in their application. A premise claiming that "if you change the cause, you'll change the effect" might be seen as a universally acceptable premise. Ultimately, though, whether a pattern of thought is acceptable depends as much on its substance as its form. We have to know something about the LDNs.

Thought pattern premises are most often employed as "warrants" in the reasoning process. They are statements which make connections between other premises, and we'll talk more about them in Chapter 9.

Stephen Toulmin has pointed out that warrants are frequently "field dependent." Whether they are acceptable or not depends upon the field we are talking about. Thus one audience or occasion may differ from another in what kinds of premises are acceptable. A legal issue may depend heavily upon argument from precedent. An audience of scientists may insist upon inductions from empirical evidence. For a religious audience, deductions based upon theological authority may be appropriate. The audience and the field determine what formal premises are acceptable and what are not.

Whom Do They Trust? "Because the New York *Times* says so" may become a premise when you are using it to create adherence to a statement which appeared in that newspaper. The written and personal sources which are trusted by the audience members provide another type of premise we may find useful in a debate.

We live not only in an information society, but in a credentialed society. Listeners will rely upon credentials, but what credentials they will trust may well vary from group to group. Sophisticated audiences may know who the experts are and respond to their names. They may know who an Alan Greenspan or a Robert Weiss is without being told. Others may have some categories of sources, such as college professors or denominational bishops, to whom they respond positively. We need to know what names they recognize and what kind of people they regard as authorities.

Knowing what documentary sources listeners will accept is necessary as well. In one public debate, a speaker made frequent references to the *New Perspectives Quarterly* as the source of her information. This left her open to the challenge that all her facts came from some place "none of us have heard of." The *New Perspectives Quarterly* is a reputable source, but the audience members are the ones who have to decide that. If there is a doubt, then you will need to provide further data to show that your source is reliable. Even the nature of the different media may be a factor, depending on whether this group sees newspapers, television, professional journals, or government documents as most acceptable.

"He's a professor of sociology at Yale" or "It appeared in *Scientific American*" will be suitable premises when you are sure that these are sources to which your audience will give credence.

Everything that the audience already knows or values will be resources for finding premises which may be used as "starting points" for argument in a debate.

WHAT ARE THEY WILLING TO ACCEPT?

Individuals who are making judgments about a public affairs question will want to know as much as possible about it in order to make reasonable decisions. You will share with the others the responsibility of bringing in premises which go beyond what they already know and believe. A good debate is a learning experience. Among the many varieties of premises listeners will normally be willing to accept as starting points for argument are fresh information, statistics, studies, and expert opinions.

Fresh Information. The new information which participants will expect to get from principal speakers and others in a debate will take such forms as "facts," descriptions, explanations, and narratives.

Facts are statements about events or conditions which are relatively subject to confirmation through observation. We can tell people that the Communication Workers are on strike, who's on the Supreme Court, or that some storm drains are tied into the sewage system. When speakers say "That's a fact," they usually are implying that their premise is undeniable, but factual statements always involve a degree of interpretation which makes them vulnerable to challenge like anything else. Still, as a speaker or listener you will frequently be saying, "Let's look at the facts."

A description of the condition of the homeless in big cities or of traffic conditions in your own community will consist of an assemblage of facts and their interpretation. Such a description may provide more useful information than "isolated" facts will.

An explanation of the beliefs of the Shi'ite Muslims or the provisions of the Roe v. Wade decision would be examples of expository support for arguments.

The fresh information may profitably be put into narrative form. We can tell the story of how the nation developed a substantial trade deficit, for instance, or how a drug addict "kicked the habit."

Notice that each of these methods of assembling factual information implies certain connections, such as causal relationships, among the facts presented. And the particular audience and situation may have a bearing upon what may and may not be accepted as facts in that debate.

Statistics. Statistics are, of course, collections of measurable data, an indispensable method for handling large amounts of factual data in public deliberation.

The simplest use of statistics is for basic classification and enumeration. How many drunk drivers are there in the United States? How many family farms? What is the average gradepoint average in your college or university?

In more sophisticated usages, statistics reveal significant relationships among the collected data. For example, they may be used to demonstrate important correlations among phenomena, as when you show that the disease rate in a community is proportional to the amount of air pollution in the atmosphere. Or they may be used to reveal differences, as when you show that two states have significantly different unemployment rates.

Statistics may also demonstrate trends of various kinds which may then be transformed into projections for the future.

Explanations of the way the statistics have been derived and handled will often be fundamental to their acceptance. The methodologies now available for drawing conclusions from statistical data are complex and sophisticated. When put into a form suitable for public decision-making, they constitute powerful premises for argumentation.

Studies. When a group wants to find out the relationship between watching violence on television and violent behavior in youths, they frequently will authorize a "study" of the matter, utilizing statistics and many other research methods. Studies and investigations of such subjects as pornography, nuclear fallout, illegal drugs, white collar crime, or foreign aid generate useful premises you can tell your listeners about. Scholarly journals are full of useful studies. The data they contain and the conclusions they arrive at are among their most helpful features.

As with stricter statistical evidence, an awareness of the research methodologies and even the possible biases of those who conduct a study is necessary in order to evaluate its strength.

Expert Opinions. Public debaters have to be able to use relevant opinions of experts as premises in their argumentation. Specialists in many technical areas provide much of the information we need in the public decision-making process. If you want to know whether the disease AIDS can be transmitted through casual contact or whether the "Star Wars" weapons system will work effectively, you turn to experts who have studied the matter and whose backgrounds and experience make their opinions worth considering.

Necessarily the opinions we use as premises must either be conclusionary in form or will be supported with a simplified rationale. This means that we will depend upon other experts to confirm or to indicate weaknesses in the conclusions or rationales presented. Where experts disagree, we employ lines of argument which support or deny the credibility of the persons we are citing, since even presumed experts can be biased or may operate beyond their actual expertise.

Reliance upon specialists does not mean giving up public judgment; it simply means being able to use the experts in the service of better decision-making. Expert opinions are indispensable elements in this process. We can hardly get along without them.

DEGREES OF ACCEPTANCE

Audience acceptance of premises is not a binary phenomenon. Listeners will agree with your premises to varying degrees. Even material you regard as factual may face "somewhat agree" rather than "strongly agree" within a latitude of acceptance. Values and opinion premises are even more subject to such fluctuations in acceptance. As you accumulate premises which you think the audience already accepts, or would be willing to accept, you take the potential degree of acceptance into consideration. The stronger the premises, the greater the potential degree of ultimate adherence to the proposition you are upholding.

Listeners may accept premises on an "until or unless" basis. They will accept an explanation of, say, the "greenhouse effect" until it is contradicted by other explanations. They may accept information they can remember having heard before until it is contradicted or they are reminded of something else. Even strong values such as "Thou shalt not kill" are generally accepted only with certain reservations. And sometimes listeners will agree to consider certain premises "for the sake of argument," waiting to see where those premises may lead.

And audiences are made up of individuals. As far as agreeing with your premises, some do and some don't. Setting forth a premise which is acceptable to some members of an audience may even have a negative impact upon other members, so the choice of what ones you'll use depends upon careful audience analysis.

Furthermore, any statement of a premise is inherently ambiguous to some extent. I may believe strongly in the idea of government "of the people, by the people, and for the people," but if you mean that every matter should be decided by popular vote, I might disagree with that. My agreement with your premise concerning pornography may depend upon what you mean by the term, pornography. Statements absorb some of their meaning from the context within which they are made, so listeners may legitimately say "it depends what you're talking about" when asked to accept a premise. No audience can be coerced into accepting a premise.

So although our agreed upon premises constitute the "starting points of argument" in a debate, these starting points are located within the minds of the audience and they will always have their variable and problematic features.

RESEARCH

All of these premises have to come from somewhere, of course. To be proficient and effective participants in public debate we have to know how to get our hands on relevant information. To make appropriate choices in our argumentation, we have to have lots of potential premises to choose from. This means research.

Research for public affairs debating has some rather special features, you will find. For instance, you'll normally be working with quite recent materials because you're usually debating timely topics, so you have to know where the recent stuff is. Public affairs research also frequently calls for going beyond library resources for information. And you will even be exploring what's in people's minds, since anything they now believe may constitute an acceptable premise in a debate.

The research process is guided by analysis and even by the clash of debate itself. The developing lines of reasoning tell us what to look for. Thus our informational horizon constantly expands.

Researching the Audience

The controlling question in public communication is "Who am I talking to?" This question influences even the search for debate premises. All along, as we look for information in all kinds of places, we keep going back to explore the situation with the intended audiences. We want to find out, in the first instance, what they already know. Evidence has been defined as what the audience believes. That doesn't mean that it can't change, just that we have to know what they know.

To some extent we can surmise what listeners will know as we look in printed sources. Note what is being said often enough so that most people will have become familiar with it. They will know about a hostage crisis or a shuttle disaster. Everybody does. Moreover, insofar as we are familiar with the persons in a particular audience we can think about what they especially know and believe.

Very specifically, this type of "research" may be carried on in conversation before the debate. Ask questions and listen. This is research, too. And even during the course of a debate you will be getting premises you can use from what other people say in their speeches and comments. Research never stops.

But we look many other places, as well, since the thorough knowledge of a subject which we expect of ourselves and others may go far beyond what most of the members of the audience already know. Our aim, then, is to know how to use the wide range of resources which is available to us.

Periodicals and Books

Sure, go to the library. On most topics print resources will give you a rich lode of information, if you know how to locate it.

Indexes. An index is a "map" of what is available. You already know how to use the library and some computerized information services, so you can go right to work on readily available material.

To dig deeper and find out the facts behind what is written in the more popular periodicals you can become familiar with the *Social Science Index*, the *Humanities Index*, and the *Public Affairs Information Service Bulletin*. Depending on the topic, there are numerous more specialized indexes to use, such as the *Education Index*, the *Business Periodicals Index*, and the *General Science Index*. These are indexes which will get you to the sophisticated academic and professional journals and other special publications which are of most use to persons discussing public affairs.

Nationally distributed newspapers, such as the *Wall Street Journal*, New York *Times*, and *Christian Science Monitor* publish regular indexes . You can also use, say, the *New York Times Index* to find articles in regional and local papers, since they all cover events when they happen.

Indexes of this kind, and others, are increasingly available as computer data bases. Most of what we could say here about computer data bases will be superseded by the time you read it.

All indexes have special features and peculiarities to get used to. To look up material on hand guns, for instance, you need to look under "firearms." It isn't our purpose here to give instructions on the use of each index, but to emphasize that knowing how to use them efficiently is important in order to have good debates.

Newspapers, Magazines, and Journals. Newspapers are naturally an important resource when debating matters of immediate concern. We need to be familiar with national papers such as those mentioned, the good regional papers, and local papers (even student newspapers) for local events. Readily available also are three widely circulated newsmagazines, *Newsweek, Time,* and *United States News and World Report.* Keep up with at least one of these.

Certain periodical publications are, because of their format, of special value to individuals concerned with public affairs. We'll note five of them.

The *Annals of the American Academy of Political and Social Science.* Each issue of the *Annals* is thematic, and it could be one of your best sources. Footnotes and bibliographies are excellent additional aids.

Congressional Digest. Each issue takes up a topic currently being debated in Congress and presents pro and con arguments concerning it. The treatment is not deep, but it provides a good introduction to any subject.

Congressional Quarterly Weekly Report. The *CQ Weekly Report* gives you a gold mine of specific facts and statistics concerning issues absorbing Congressional attention, with background essays and cross-referencing.

Congressional Record. This is basically a record of all the debate in both houses of Congress, plus a daily section of "Extensions of Remarks" for supplemental materials inserted by Congress members. There's a lot of garbage in the *Congressional Record*, but also some substantial articles and arguments. The *Congressional Record* has its own index.

Current History. Each issue has a theme related to foreign affairs questions. Articles are authoritative and well-documented.

To explore a full range of opinions and to be exposed to evidence you may not find elsewhere, you can look at a wide range of "opinion" magazines, such as *Christian Century, Commentary, Commonweal, Nation, National Review, New Republic,* and *The Progressive.* You may find useful some of the ideas of the far left, the far right, and the far out.

A huge variety of academic and professional journals, such as *Foreign Affairs Quarterly,* will provide more reliable and documented material for use as acceptable premises in a debate.

Books. And we certainly don't want to slight books as a resource. If the topic you are debating has been around for a while, relevant books and monographs will have appeared and will be available in a library or book store. Sometimes edited volumes of studies related to a particular topic are especially useful. Check the handy card or electronic catalog.

Libraries also have reference sections (and reference staff members) where encyclopedias, statistical data, reports, and collections are located to give you quick information access.

Government Documents

Once you get the hang of finding them, government publications are indispensable sources of information about public policy questions.

U. S. Government documents have their own rather unwieldy numbering and indexing system, and you ought to learn to use it if you haven't already done so. The basic index you use to locate these materials is the *United States Government Publications Monthly Catalog* or its electronic cousin. When you find an item that looks useful in the *Monthly Catalog* subject index, it will have a number which looks something like this: Y 4.Ag: D 34/pt. 2. You can then locate the publication in your library, order it from the Superintendent of Documents, or write to a Congressperson for assistance.

Congressional hearings and committee reports provide material on a wide variety of matters of public concern.

Special Interest Groups

There's an amazing amount of information which hardly anybody knows about. Normally of interest to a limited number of persons, this information is collected and disseminated by a vast array of special interest groups and societies. You can find addresses for many of them, ranging from the National Rifle Association to the American Society of Dowsers, in magazine rack reference books such as the *World Almanac*. Even more organizations are listed in the *Encyclopedia of Associations,* which you can find in the library reference sections noted above.

You've also heard of "think tanks." These are research institutions whose main purpose is to generate documented and scholarly studies of public problems. Among the most productive of these are the Brookings Institution and the American Enterprise Institute, both in Washington, D.C.

You can write or call any of these organizations to obtain a list of their available publications or even to get specific pieces of information you may need.

The whole idea of the research process is to expand the scope of premises which may be acceptable to audiences and to create a fuller understanding of the many ramifications of a topic.

STORAGE AND RETRIEVAL

So far we have been exploring how to retrieve data from the information storage systems available to us in this information age. While we are conducting this exploration, we also have to be setting up our own personal storage and retrieval system.

One of the inherent characteristics of public debate is an "immediacy" factor, and the immediacy factor affects the research process along with everything else. Most of the topics we debate publicly are of immediate concern, which means that a person needs to be able to find very recent information, find it quickly, and have it ready for timely use.

Taking Notes. Because of the immediacy factor, you probably should not get too bogged down in taking notes. "Don't take notes; take nickels." Photocopying is often a dime or more rather than a nickel these days, but the substantial advantages of photocopying remain the same. It's faster than copying by hand or on a typewriter and it usually provides you with a fuller context for the facts or opinions you wish to record. Oh, all right, you can take a few notes when you have an isolated quotation or general idea you want to jot down from an article not worth more attention, or when the duplicating facilities aren't handy.

If you are jotting notes by hand, it's all right to paraphrase, too. If you read that private industry is hesitant to get into the space launch business even though given the "green light" to do so, you can make a note of that conclusion without copying the whole article. Public debates seldom get down to quibbles about exact quotations.

Careful documentation, however, still remains an important habit. Whether you are photocopying, jotting notes, or taking down quotations, keep an exact record of where you are getting your ideas. This practice allows you to go back and review material or to meet challenges to your information when they are posed.

Some persons who debate are infatuated with 4x6 cards and like to transform all of their notes into a form suitable for a card file. This system is not especially suitable for most public debate. It's all right if you plan to have 100 debates and have plenty of time and help. Even then, partitioning material into snippets of evidence tends to lead one away from major patterns and issues. A public debate is not ordinarily an "evidence war" and reading quantities of material from cards may lead to gentle mockery rather than adherence of the audience to your position. At best, a modest collection of carefully filed items may be a helpful supplement to your other evidence.

Indexing and Retrieving. With your accumulations of photocopies, clippings, magazines, and notes, you will normally construct an index to lead you quickly to whatever you'll need during the debate. This index, which might be several pages long, will probably follow the topical analysis you have developed. It should be keyed to tabs and titles on the material itself. Some articles will have premises relating to several different points, of course.

If you are preparing a "principal" speech for a debate, you have time to go through your material at a relatively leisurely pace. However, in the course of an actual debate you have to be able to find things quickly. (Or even better, have them in your head. Your short and long range memory are, after all, an important part of your filing system.) Avoid clogging your files with arcane, peripheral or unduly redundant items. Just take what you think you'll need. Then be as familiar as possible with that material and have an indexing system, perhaps using letter and number symbols, which will lead you quickly to what you want. Most audiences do not want to wait around while you take a long time to find your facts.

As we will see when we talk about clash, some materials may be put together in the form of "blocks," so that several related facts or opinions are pre-organized on one sheet of paper for use when they become relevant.

In the end, you have to find out what works for you. However you do it, efficient storage and retrieval of information will be a vital part of what you do, even as a listener, in a public debate.

Chapter 8

Testing the Premises

We have referred to the premises we have been accumulating as the "starting points of argument." From now on, all kinds of things can happen to these premises as speakers and audiences move along the road toward new decisions. We're looking at a huge "process area" which exists between the premises we offer and the propositions to which we are seeking adherence.

One of the events which may take place in that process area is the further testing of any problematic premises, even to the point of making once accepted premises doubtful in the minds of the audience. Another event along the reasoning road is the patterning and combining of the premises to produce relationships and inferences leading to a conclusion. And we may also find that during this process we will be adjusting in various ways the impact and even the meaning of the premises we have accepted.

THE TOULMIN MODEL

British philosopher Stephen Toulmin has presented us with a helpful "model" of the reasoning process which will clarify some of the things that go on in the process area.

One important observation which Toulmin made is that the

reasoning process for most of the issues we really argue about is more "judicial" than "mathematical." That means that although we can put the matter into a form which makes our reasoning easier to do, only through our own personal judgment can we decide whether the conclusion is acceptable. A second fundamental observation is that we normally argue in rather ordinary language and have to have ways to evaluate reasoning that is expressed in such everyday language. The Toulmin model permits us to analyze and evaluate reasoning that is expressed in ordinary language so long as we can identify the elements which he has described.

Of special interest to us will be five features of his model, namely, (1) the claim, (2) data, (3) the warrant, (4) the reservation, and (5) the qualifier. Note that each of these labels represents a function which a statement might serve. When a statement stands as a "claim," it is a proposition which is yet to be proven. When it is identified as "data," it is the basic point from which the reasoning process starts. A statement which functions as a "warrant" tells why the claim follows from the data. A "reservation" is an exception to the warrant. A "qualifier" designates the strength of the claim being made. Thus, any premise, such as "High inflation is harmful to persons on fixed incomes," might be data in one debate, a warrant in another, a reservation in a third, and might even be a claim at times.

When we analyze a line of reasoning into these elements, we can more systematically evaluate whether we want to accept that reasoning. As usual, it is ultimately up to human individuals to decide whether the statements contained in the reasoning add up to the conclusion, or "claim," which we or someone else is advocating.

Let's look at a simple example.

Data: An American jetliner was blown up by terrorists.
Warrant: (Since) If this happens once, it could happen many times.
Reservation: (Unless) This kind of event can be stopped by precautionary methods.
Claim: (So) Terrorist activities pose a serious threat.
Qualifier: Quite likely.

Taking such an example, we can evaluate the argument by asking a number of questions about each part of the model. We can, for instance, ask a question about the acceptability of the premises stated in the data, the warrant, and the reservation. We can see whether the warrant authorizes an inferential leap to the claim. (We'll come back to that phrase, "inferential leap," in Chapter 9.) And finally, we can note the impact of the reservations on the force of the total argument. Let's take a fuller look at each one of these steps. As we do so, of course, we may continually modify the analysis we earlier arrived at and will be seeking out new premises as we need them during our excursion through the process area.

In this chapter we will be looking for ways to test the acceptability of premises, whether they are used in a particular instance as data, or as warrants, or as reservations. Chapter 9 will explore the ways in which warrants work.

CHALLENGING DATA

So now we go to work. Since any line of argument is derived from agreed-upon premises which function as "data," we begin by determining whether any of this data should be challenged or tested before we go further. Do we have our facts right? Do other people have their information straight?

Premises which function as data in an argument are commonly referred to as "evidence," so it is what we all think of as evidence that we are talking about here. Still, the tests we will suggest are equally applicable to premises which serve functions other than data. In all cases we want to know whether the statements are acceptable as we proceed with the debate.

If we are members of an audience at a public debate, we will challenge evidence in order to make our judgments more rational. If we are advocates proposing the acceptance of a proposition, we will want to satisfy ourselves that we are right and that the facts we are using meet our own standards, and obviously if we are on the opposing side we have every motive and obligation to test those premises as thoroughly as possible.

As we know, there is no absolute way to be sure that a fact or any other premise is "true." The best we can do is to make a human judgment that the premise is acceptable enough to be used as a starting point and to allow us to go ahead with our reasoning process. In any event, acceptance or rejection of evidentiary statements is hardly a completely binary process, as you will recall, and thus there are degrees of acceptance within an audience. And naturally, some members of an audience may be willing to accept evidence which other members completely reject.

A good deal of the information presented in public debate is acceptable enough to serve its purpose as a starting point. We don't have to be completely suspicious of every fact that is presented to us.

Still, debating is a critical process and we are obligated to keep our eyes open. And there will be times when we should indeed "blow the whistle" on some of the premises we are asked to accept. Therefore we can learn to ask certain kinds of questions about these premises and use them as a guide for locating deficiencies (and strengths) of the evidence in a debate. The questions are guidelines for human judgment.

We will look at a few of the questions which one might ask about any premise set forth in argument, then look further at some special categories of evidentiary premises such as empirical information, statistics, and expert opinions and see what questions we might ask about them.

All Evidence. Whenever we identify a premise we will make quick judgments about it, stopping for greater scrutiny whenever substantial doubts are raised by the answers to these questions. This procedure does not mean going through complex intellectual maneuvers or stopping the debate to question everything in sight. It just means, "Look out." Five basic and useful questions are these:

(1) Is the evidence consistent with other evidence?

(2) Is the evidence precise enough for our purposes?

(3) Would the evidence be subject to verification?

(4) Is the evidence applicable to the realm of discourse at hand?

(5) Has the evidence been taken out of context?

Consistency is a primary standard. If evidence does not fit with the other things we know about or with what we regard as probable, we will want to stop and take another look at it. When a speaker says, "In 1985, 91 percent of the occupants killed in auto accidents were not wearing seatbelts," we may accept this statement as a fact because it seems reasonable and no one has told us otherwise. If the figure given were 5 percent, we might be more doubtful.

Naturally, if anyone introduces explicitly contradictory evidence into a debate, we are back to square one. An inconsistency has been introduced and it will have to be resolved before we go further. On the other hand, with nothing apparently contradictory, we may simply go ahead without further worry.

Verifiability as a standard for evidence of any kind means that we can check it out if we want to. If an assertion is such that we have to take it or leave it, we may want to resist its acceptance. We might more quickly question an assertion about the intentions of the Castro government in Cuba, since they would be hard to confirm, than one about the foreign sources of oil in the United States.

Similarly, applicability within a realm of discourse will be a standard we should apply in some cases. A dream or a "hunch" might be useful in making a decision about betting on a horse race, but should be dismissed immediately when choosing among political candidates. On a scientific proposition, evidence taken from historical novels may possibly be dismissed as irrelevant. In a state public service commission hearing on rate increases for a utility company, where the standard being examined is simply profit margin, testimony from persons who are freezing in their homes is often simply disregarded, no matter how true. As we know, in courtroom situations, certain kinds of evidence are legally inadmissible. We ask whether the data is suited to this conversation.

Most quotations, and even facts and statistics, gain meaning from the context in which they appear and thus may need to be questioned when they appear in a new context. More than one advocate has been known to take quotations out of context.

Empirical Information. Using information which is a product of direct observation is like having a witness in a court case. Individuals have observed rural poverty in Putnam County, street riots in Chicago in 1968, or wing vibrations on an Air Force T-46 trainer. Such evidence is highly valued by social scientists, who are most systematically concerned with the kinds of subjects ordinarily debated in public. Empirical data have the virtue of being confirmable through the agreement of observers who are reporting it. Still, we will want to be ready to ask questions to see whether any warning flags emerge to make us cautious about such evidence. Some of these questions are:

(1) Was the observer qualified to observe the phenomena?

(2) Was the observer in a position to make the observation?

(3) Is the description of the situation or occurrence unduly biased?

These questions address the fact that observations of social phenomena are much more difficult to control than scientific occurrences. People see even the "same" events from different perspectives and describe them in different words.

The first two questions help us examine the accuracy of the facts. Sometimes the reporter didn't know enough about the subject to be able to recognize what was going on and in some cases wasn't there at all. Frequently it takes an experienced and knowledgeable observer to be able to describe something, and the observer has to be where the action is in order to report it reliably.

The third question will suggest to us that even experienced observers may be biased and tend to "slant" their descriptions. The descriptions made of the same incident by a police official and by a "protester" may be quite different.

We may have to do a good deal of surmising in addressing such questions. Most of the time these facts are presented without an indication of who the observers actually were. In critical cases, we may have to ask about that as well.

Statistics. Statistics, which were mentioned in Chapter 7 as another form of evidence which audiences may be willing to accept, are accumulations of quantified data, and their treatment is vital in most public debate. Public policy questions almost always involve lots of cases, and we have to have some way to get beyond the individual instance and look at the whole picture. Statistics is our tool.

As usual, caution is required in accepting or rejecting statistical evidence. One intriguing little book on the subject is called *How to Lie with Statistics,*. revealing many of the hazards involved in the ordinary use of statistics. A popular remark says, there are three kinds of evidence, "lies, damn lies, and statistics."

We have to use statistics in public debate, and we have to use them in a manageable form, so knowing some of the questions to ask ourselves and others when they appear is imperative.

(1) Are appropriate base lines used for the figures?

(2) Are the methods of statistical manipulation appropriate for this use of the data?

(3) Are the units of measurement comparable?

Base lines will make a big difference. For instance, the deficit of the Federal Government may look horrendous when compared with 25 years ago, but may be seen as "improving" if compared with last year. Federal spending on Veterans Affairs may have decreased in percentages, but because the total budget was skyrocketing will have in reality increased in dollar amounts. Most statistical evidence involves projections or comparisons. Just what is it, then, that you are comparing things with? What are you basing your projections upon?

If you have had a course in statistics, or even studied them as part of a course, you know that there are many ways to process figures. You know that there are differences between means, medians and modes. You know that you can figure variations and correlations. The description of statistical methods is beyond the scope of this book, but within your knowledge and the knowledge of your audience. Questions of statistical methodology should be routinely raised to see whether caution is justified regarding the acceptance of the data presented.

And how are the units being measured? All statistics translate experience into quantifiable units of some kind. When measuring popular attitudes, for instance, we may be using an attitude scale of some kind or may be asking yes or no questions. We may simply be counting letters to congressmen. A figure which gives one impression when expressed in absolute terms may give a far different one when set forth in percentages. Asking ourselves and others about these units may tell us whether or not to accept the figures being given to us.

One other thing, while we're talking about statistics. The very form in which the statistics are presented to the audience may involve some hazards. On visual aids, for instance. If the chart is tall and narrow, the unemployment figures climb alarmingly. If the chart is flat and low, it creeps up slowly, so far as we can see. The presentation as well as the calculation of statistical figures may be important elements in proof for a public audience.

Statistics regarding matters of public concern are frequently the result of "studies" of various kinds. Our questions regarding the acquisition and processing of data should then be applied to the methodology of the whole study. Studies are usually conducted by groups or individuals who are operating in specialized fields, so some familiarity with the research techniques of those fields is very helpful. You have to know how terms were defined and how data were accumulated. Were there, for instance, interviews or questionnaires? How were phenomena measured? And, of course, how adequate were the statistical manipulations?

Expert Opinions. Public debate is highly dependent upon the opinions and judgments of authoritative experts who have studied the matters being debated. While audiences cannot simply abandon important public matters to "experts" to decide, they must make the best possible use of all the resources available to them. They must learn how to use expert opinion. Where experts frequently cannot explain to laymen the basis of opinions which are derived, perhaps, from years of experience, the public has to decide just how expert the opinion actually is. As with the evaluation of other kinds of evidence, there is no infallible measuring rod for such data, only a set of questions which might guide us:

(1) Is the expert qualified in the field in which he or she is testifying?

(2) Is the authority relatively impartial and unbiased?

(3) Is the opinion cited as evidence taken in context?

The first two questions, regarding the qualifications and impartiality of the authority, are especially important. Our very acceptance or rejection of the data is based not upon the examination of the facts and reasoning but upon what this person thinks. We have to trust him or her. As a technical matter, the qualifications of the expert are the data we are examining; the actual statement is only a claim until these are established. Some persons who make impressive statements are not qualified, or are not qualified in the field they are talking about. Others have full credentials, but they work for organizations with special interests or have biases which reduce their credibility. We have to remain alert to such circumstances.

Sometimes the experts come in an institutional cover, and our evaluation of even statistical studies must be based upon the source. Senator Glenn informs his colleagues that "NASA states that we have gotten back in benefit to our economy $7 for every dollar we have spent." He himself then cautions, "Let us say NASA is over exuberant in their study...."

In a partisan endeavor such as a debate, some advocates are tempted to take quotations out of context, like the blurbs in movie ads. Even when the quotations are exact and the intentions are good, the evidence is naturally forced into condensed form for public consumption and full context is almost impossible to provide. This check point will permit us to be aware of such a possibility in evaluating evidence.

Documentary Sources. Audiences who are making judgments about matters of public concern will justifiably assent to data which are derived from newspaper and magazine sources they regard as trustworthy. Certain questions can then be asked about these sources:

(1) Is the documentary source known to be objective?

(2) Where a source of information is slanted, are we able to make allowances for this?

(3) Is all of the evidence derived from a single source?

(4) Have intermediate sources affected the selection and interpretation of the evidence?

Both relatively objective and relatively biased sources may be used, so long as we know what we're doing. Sometimes a biased source is the only place to find out certain information. And no source is likely to be completely impartial. Different audiences will have respect for different publications and, as usual, we can only ask the questions we need to ask and leave it to the judgment of audiences as to the reliability of our documentary sources. Even when we are making our own judgments, we will have to rely to some extent on our past experience and the reputation the periodical, or even the medium, has earned.

The danger of relying upon a single source is that we have little to compare the material with. Whenever we hear a stream of evidence from only one source, our question-asking powers should snap into play. Everyone concerned might well be looking for an additional basis for accepting or rejecting the premises having narrow support..

We can remember that everyone in the debate may be asking these questions about empirical data, statistics, expert opinions and sources, so this examination is, like everything else, a shared process. We may notice also that many of the types of premises described in Chapter 7, such as values and assumptions, have not been mentioned yet. They may be less subject to "tests of evidence," but still require review before acceptance.

VALUES AND COMMON SENSE

As you may have noticed, some of the important kinds of premises we talked about in the last chapter, such as "values" and "world views"," are not always thought of as forms of evidence. Yet since these ideas and assumptions frequently function as vital starting points upon which audience agreement is to be assumed, they also should be "checked out" by advocates, opponents and listeners. Are these premises worth giving our assent to?

In an audience debate, a value statement such as "all men are created equal" may be as self-evident as the fact that the sun rises every morning. We can then use it as a starting point for argument just as the founding fathers did in the Declaration of Independence or Abraham Lincoln did in his Gettysburg Address. It's an acceptable premise.

If the statement is not acceptable, or on the basis of preliminary scrutiny constitutes a matter of dispute, it is no longer a starting point or premise but rather a debatable claim which must itself be argued about on the basis of reasoning and other more acceptable evidence. In the process of testing premises we try to assess the extent to which such argumentation is necessary or whether the given premise is sufficiently acceptable to go on with the debate.

Values. Values are essentially judgments concerning what is preferable, what is right and what is wrong, what is good and what is evil. Such values as honesty, fairness, patriotism, the family, individualism, education and (the big one in much public debate) liberty frequently serve as basic premises in our discourse. As suggested in an earlier chapter, a central value concern often provides a basis for the whole debate. Not all values are positive, of course, so you can use negative values like ugliness, social isolation, or crabgrass as premises as well.

Whether to accept any premise is a judgment call. Some questions can help us to decide about the acceptability of values which we or others are using as premises in a debate.

(1) Is the value contradicted or superseded by an opposing value?

(2) Is the value appropriately applied to its context?

(3) Is the value as stated clear enough to the audience to be meaningful in a speech?

The first test, then, is to juxtapose other values to the one being advocated. Most values have "opposites" which may be considered, or higher counterparts which may reduce their acceptability. Faced with an assertion of the value of "justice," a speaker would not necessarily counter with the idea that injustice is a good thing, but might dwell on the quality of mercy, frequently in conflict with justice. If you give a person his or her "just deserts," you do not at the same time extend great generosity. The test of the value is to ask whether, given a constellation of possible values, one still maintains the original one.

Value arguments depend to some extent on context, also, so we try to guard against an inappropriate application. We may value the "family," for instance, but still be wary when we are asked to treat an organization, a corporation, or a nation as a family.

As values are notoriously and necessarily abstract, undue ambiguity will lead to confusing argument. At times such terms as "equality" and "liberty" may become almost meaningless unless defined clearly in a speech. We don't accept it as a premise until we know for sure what it means.

"Common Sense." Public debate depends upon a vast store of accumulated popular knowledge which is available to debaters as premises in argument. And even common sense should be spot-checked for acceptability so far as you can do it.

Common sense takes a number of forms. In the preceding chapter we mentioned "world views," tendencies to look at the world as a battleground of conflicting forces, or to see the progress of civilization as inevitable, or to see mankind as guided by Divine purpose. A world view is one kind of common sense.

Another form of usable wisdom consists of what are sometimes called "cultural myths." (The word "myth" doesn't necessarily mean the idea isn't true.) Anyway, such myths as "the American dream" and that "we can solve any problem if we roll up our sleeves and get to work" are always available as premises. A third form you might think of is "aphoristic wisdom," ranging from "you get what you pay for" to "I am my brother's keeper." And fourthly, let's keep in mind that public discourse rests on a substantial groundwork of "reasonable assumptions," such as that people on fixed incomes are hurt by inflation or simply that normal happenings will go on occurring.

Since even common sense and common knowledge require scrutiny, there are a several questions which may be helpful in checking these out as well.

(1) Does the idea stand up when translated into clear propositional form?

(2) How universal is its acceptance?

(3) Is it applicable to the case at hand?

The "cherry tree myth" is undoubtedly an artifact of our national culture, but since it is not literally true, we need to ask what it is really saying. For instance, we might transform it into "the founding fathers had high moral standards" and see whether we would still accept it. Most of us would be willing to do so.

Some wisdom is popular only within limited groups. A possible test of an assumption, then, might reasonably be the degree to which it is widely believed. The answer to the question of whether most people agree that students don't work hard enough in school might help us as speakers or listeners to decide whether we should accept it as fact.

In a Congressional debate on space exploration, generally acceptable common sense pops up continually. "Whenever nations work together they will not be fighting each other," is one statement. "Scientific leadership means political leadership," is another you might see. We simply ask whether these statements are meaningful and applicable in this particular debate.

In summary, human values and common knowledge provide as

much a base for public argument as do documented sources and specialized facts, so a critical approach is necessary to every premise we hear in a debate. The questions we ask about these premises will help us decide whether to plunge ahead with our speech or to stop and think about it some more.

Chapter 9

The Warranting Process

In order "to create or increase adherence of audiences to propositions," there has to be a mental "movement" of some kind between what audiences already believe and what they are being asked to accept. In their minds they have to engage in a warranting process which will lead from data to a claim.

Stephen Toulmin divided argumentation into two steps, first asking "What have you got to go on?" and following with a second question, "How do you get there?" In talking about data, we've been asking "What have you got to go on?" Now we'll think about how we "Get there." What goes on in our minds as we draw conclusions from the data we have accepted?

As we saw in the last chapter, Toulmin gave the name "warrant" to a premise which authorizes a step in the direction of a claim or conclusion. Warrants consist of rules, principles, "inference-licenses," etc. They are statements you'd use to answer the question of how you get to a certain conclusion from accepted data. Let's take an example. Say the audience has accepted the following fact.

(DATA) The wages of manufacturing workers in Brazil are 10% of what they are in the United States.

One claim which might then be accepted on the basis of that fact is that

(CLAIM) The United States government should put high tariffs on manufactured goods from Brazil.

To answer the question of "How did you get there?" you might offer a statement of the following kind:

(WARRANT) The government should use tariffs to compensate for unfair wage competition.

As indicated, that statement is a warrant, and if it is acceptable it gives the audience a reason for adhering to the claim.

The tricky part of this reasoning process is that you can come up with differing and even contradictory conclusions from a single piece of data. All you have to do is change the warrant. Using the same piece of data as above, the same "fact" about wage rates in Brazil, you could conceivably make a claim which is the exact opposite of the one we came up with before:

(NEW CLAIM) The government should NOT place high tariffs on manufactured goods from Brazil.

If we are asked the question, "How in the world did you get to a conclusion completely contrary to the one you drew before?" we can cite a warrant to the following effect:

(NEW WARRANT) American consumers should be allowed the benefit of the cheapest goods anyone is willing to produce.

You can make up these thinking tricks, "trinks," for yourself, if you wish. Reverse the result. Someone might reason, for example, that "Siwash University has high academic standards, so therefore you should try to get admitted there." That's reasonable enough if your warrant is that one should attend a university with high academic standards. But to someone who accepts the warrant, "I want easy grades," the conclusion might be "DON'T try to get admitted to Siwash."

At this point, before we consider the ways we might test the warrants we use, let's pause and note five special characteristics these "inference-licenses" have.

Remember, for one thing, that these thinking processes are taking place within individuals who are part of your audience. You can't detach them from what the listeners actually believe. A multitude of listeners will have a multitude of thinking patterns, depending for one thing upon what warrants they are willing to accept and how they apply these warrants in specific situations.

Facts don't speak for themselves; people do. Notice that the acceptability of the warrants introduced in the above reasoning about tariffs will depend to some extent upon whether the listeners identify themselves with workers or with consumers.

Secondly, the reasoning that takes place in public debate is conducted in the ordinary kind of language which people use. The warrants employed may be stated in many different forms. We are not talking about an exact mathematics-type calculation, but about lines of thought which seem generally acceptable to thinking individuals.

Furthermore (3), the account we have been giving has been considerably simplified over what happens in most debates. For instance, a multitude of pieces of data may be combined in many forms in a given situation, so we usually are not working with just one item of data, one warrant, and one claim. And not every element of the reasoning process is stated explicitly.

Fourthly, the warrant, especially, is frequently left unstated until someone finds it necessary to bring it up. Still, our ability to identify and evaluate these functions for ourselves and our listeners is central to public debate.

Finally, the term warrant is applied to the function of a statement. A given premise, like the one saying that "the government should use tariffs to compensate for unfair wage competition," may be a warrant in one case, but a claim, a datum, or even a reservation in another. A statement functions as a warrant when it authorizes an inferential leap.

EVALUATING WARRANTS

We all like to have things make sense to us. We want our thinking to be reasonable. And in a public debate our thinking has to seem reasonable to other people besides ourselves. There is very little thinking on important matters which is universally valid, but we can ask some questions to guide ourselves and others into common sense conclusions.

As we have noticed, the key to making any inferential leap from evidence to conclusion is the warrant. So now we are going to try to classify some different types of warrants and see what questions we ask when we are using (either presenting or hearing) them.

Frankly, you can't do much reasoning if you don't know what you're talking about. To check the quality and acceptability of an inference requires a certain amount of knowledge of your topic. Just as your ability to evaluate the relevance and acceptability of data depends on what you know already, so do the relevance and acceptability of the warrant and the warranting process. You don't know whether you are making a "hasty generalization" about, say, prison conditions until you know something about the subject as a whole.

The formal classification of arguments that we're going to look at now simply provides some guidelines for individual thought. These questions help us to see whether we have covered all the bases.

We'll look specifically at five patterns of reasoning: deduction, generalization, causal reasoning, correlation, and analogy. For each pattern we'll consider the questions which are useful in evaluating the applicability of warrants which are of that type.

Deduction. For our purposes, deduction will refer to the process by which we move mentally from the general to the specific. If we have an acceptable general statement, we can make an inference concerning a specific instance of it. For instance, we may accept a general statement that "each person should be responsible for his or her own actions." If we then classify an individual who is inebriated as a "person," we may conclude that a drunk must be held accountable for any damage he or she causes while driving. We have reasoned from a general premise to its application in a specific case.

The warrant in deductive reasoning will state that what is true of all of the members of a class of phenomena is true in a particular instance of it.

Notice that just setting forth a deductive line of reasoning does not completely close the case, though. Someone else may use the same premise to say that the bartender who sold the drinks should be responsible for his actions, too. When you are debating a proposition such as "Bartenders should be held responsible for the subsequent actions of their customers," you can hear both lines of reasoning (both valid deductions) in contention with one another.

In public debate, audience members will have a stock of relatively universal generalizations which they will in the first instance tend to apply deductively to any new proposition or claim. Questions respecting the applicability of these generalizations are especially appropriate with respect to such reasoning.

In any event, among the questions we will ask ourselves and others when we recognize a warranting process as moving deductively, from the general to the specific, are these:

Is the case being considered a legitimate instance of the general statement offered as a warrant in its support?

Is the general statement sufficient to establish the claim?

And to answer these questions usually takes a knowledge of the field we are talking about.

You may be familiar with formal syllogistic logic, with its famous example of

Socrates is a man.
All men are mortal.
Therefore, Socrates is mortal.

The effort to apply abstract formal laws of reasoning is interesting and valuable. If you know how to apply them in public debating situations, fine. However, formal logic takes so much adaptation and translation to make it useful for our purposes that we will not treat it here. We'll simply ask if the reasoning we are doing makes sense when we ask the relevant questions.

Generalization, A generalization (or induction) works in the opposite intellectual direction, moving from specific instances to general statements. For example, if the audience knows about two instances of international terrorism, say a ship hi-jacking and a hostage situation, they may be willing to accept the generalization that such terrorism is widespread.

In order to test the reasonableness of a generalization, we normally ask questions such as these:

Are there enough examples or instances?

Are these examples representative?

Have negative instances been accounted for?

Again, we can't really answer these questions without knowing something about the field under discussion, but we can say things like "that's just one example" or "that example isn't at all typical." These questions can guide us toward the appropriate matters to consider.

Causal Reasoning. When we use causal reasoning, of course, we contend that a causal link exists between two or more phenomena. One thing causes another. This link is asserted in the warrant.

Causal reasoning can work in two directions, namely, from cause to effect and from effect to cause.

If we work from cause to effect, we use as data a known phenomenon and as a claim the asserted effect. If we have as data the fact that factories are letting off particle emissions in Columbus, Ohio, we may conclude that as an effect some forests in Pennsylvania will be harmed. Our warrant in such a case would be the causal link, "polluted air causes harm to forests."

We can use the same warrant to move from effect to cause. We now have as data a certain effect, that some forests are deteriorating. We then conclude, effect to cause, that there is a great amount of factory emission in the air.

The kinds of questions we will ask when we recognize an example of causal reasoning include these:

Are there other causes for the asserted effect?

Are there other effects from the asserted cause?

How strong or direct is the causal connection?

Controversy over causation is frequently central to debates on public policy questions. When we look at the dramatic decrease in highway deaths when the wearing of seatbelts was required, we are led to conclude that not wearing belts causes more deaths. However, there were advocates who asked themselves about cause and wondered whether some other factor such as higher gasoline prices, better highways, better cars, or better education may not have been the "real" cause. Such considerations reopen the argument, though we may still be permitted to conclude that our original surmise was right in the first place. Seatbelts save lives.

Correlations. Sometimes we know that two phenomena usually go together even though we can't say that one causes the other. In individual cases this is known as "sign" reasoning, where the presence of one thing is an indication of the presence of another. We recognize that a person wearing a kilt is probably Scottish, even without exploring what the causal link is.

Correlations are most frequently used statistically. For a long time an inverse statistical correlation persisted between inflation and unemployment. We concluded that to lower inflation would mean to raise unemployment. Then we had a period when both unemployment and inflation were high, so we had to reexamine the warrant and the conclusions we drew from it.

If you have studied statistics you have some notion of the relatively complex procedures employed to compute correlations and to measure their significance. Such data can be most useful in public debate so long as they can be explained coherently. Many generally recognized correlations, such as between crime and poverty, may be used as warrants without as much examination, though.

In any event, when faced with reasoning based upon correlations, there are questions you will ask.

Is the correlation significant?

Is the correlation an accidental one?

These questions guide us in checking the warrant and its applicability before we accept the conclusion.

Analogy. In using a purported analogy as a warrant, we say that when two cases are alike in many respects, they may be alike in a further respect known to exist in one case, but not in the other.

The issue is sometimes an important one in debates over banning handguns. England and Sweden, for instance, ban private possession of handguns and have substantially fewer murders. So does Japan. It may be argued that the United States is like England and Sweden, so banning handguns here would lead to a similar lack of murders.

When you have an argument from analogy, you can ask questions such as these:

Are the two cases sufficiently alike in significant respects?

Are there other factors which affect the situation?

In the case of Japan, in the above example, some advocates argue that it is cultural differences and not the banning of handguns which are the key factor. The cultures are not alike in significant respects.

Furthermore, in testing some other analogical reasoning, we might agree that the likenesses are there all right, but we would see some key differences which might tend to invalidate the conclusion.

FALLACIES

The term "fallacy" designates a substantial weakness in the warranting process. In formal logic, fallacious reasoning will completely invalidate a conclusion, but in informal logic and public debating generally, a fallacy simply constitutes a dubious chain of argument.

Any weakness in reasoning may be called a fallacy, but some of these deficiencies are blatant and frequent enough in public debates that they should be routinely recognized by participants. These potential flaws are something to look out for in the arguments which are addressed to us as listeners and even in our own thinking about a proposition. And if we can detect an apparent fallacy in the reasoning of an opponent we can triumphantly label it as such and bring it to the attention of others.

Naturally, most of us don't utter fallacies on purpose. We at least feel that there is some logic in what we're saying, and there's probably some logic in what the other person is saying as well. Fallacies are never completely fallacious. Therefore the contention that reasoning is fallacious is itself a contention, subject to affirmation or denial.

If you construct a formal syllogism such as (1) All students interested in public affairs subscribe to *Time* Magazine, (2) Jack subscribes to *Time* Magazine, and therefore (3) Jack is interested in public affairs, you would be committing the formal fallacy of the "excluded middle." Still, your reasoning might lead you to a proper conclusion.

We have already mentioned "hasty generalizations." They might be hasty, but they usually have some degree of strength to them. When we encounter generalizations, we have to be ready to examine them and decide just how "hasty" they really are.

Let's take a look at nine other fallacies which might be recognized by many audience members.

Post Hoc Ergo Propter Hoc. This is a Latin phrase meaning "after this, therefore because of this." Even though a crime wave may have occurred after a new city administration was elected, that doesn't mean that the crime wave was caused by the new administration. Still, remember that fallacies have some truth to them, so this causal connection might be worth checking out anyway.

Slippery Slope. The warrant in a "slippery slope" suggests that a small step in a certain direction will lead to a long slide. If we allow government regulation of pension plans, say, we soon will have government running everything.

Ad Hominem. Another Latin term, in its popular usage this means attacking the person making an argument rather than the argument itself.

Straw "Man." The "straw man" is a refutational warrant in which one attributes to opponents a line of argument which they themselves don't use, usually a weak argument which can be easily answered.

Red Herring. In this case, a speaker insists upon dwelling upon a minor argument which has little significance for the question at hand.

Ad Ignorantiam. Another Latin term, this time referring to an argument based upon the receiver's ignorance. "You don't know any criminals who have been rehabilitated, do you?" does not mean that none have been rehabilitated. The audience just isn't familiar with them.

Special Pleading. Some advocates are willing to employ warrants which they would not accept if other persons used them.

Non Sequitur. "It does not follow." This fallacy is an all-purpose label for claims which are simply not at all justified by the warrant introduced.

Begging the Question. An advocate who begs the question simply employs a restatement of a contention (often in different words) as grounds for accepting it. The warrant is in effect not different from the claim.

Each of these so-called fallacies serves as a warning bell that some feature of the warranting process should be examined more closely, and in many cases the argument may be dismissed under such examination. The handiest use of fallacies is as shorthand labels to apply to the reasoning of others.

QUALIFIERS AND RESERVATIONS

So far we have asked Toulmin's two questions, "What do you have to go on?" and "How did you get there?" Now we'll consider a third question to ask as we work with the premises at our disposal: "What's slowing us up?"

Do we have to modify our claims?

We have to remind ourselves that public debate is a matter of probabilities and of degrees of acceptance and adherence. You don't say "this fact is either true or false," and you don't insist that "my conclusion is either logical or it's not logical." Even within a given audience there will be a range of differences in this acceptance or adherence.

To reinforce this probabilistic notion, we can pay some attention to the function of two other elements of the Toulmin model we described in the preceding chapter, namely the "qualifier" and the "reservations." (Toulmin used the word "rebuttal" instead of "reservation," but other people have been calling them reservations.)

A qualifier is "some explicit reference to the degree of force which our data confer on our claim in virtue of our warrant," according to Toulmin. More often than not it is not even explicit.

If we indicate that our claim is "probably" acceptable or "very highly likely," we are giving an explicit statement of the degree of force which we think our claim has. When we are considering claims made by other participants in the debate, we may well want to clarify for ourselves and others just how forceful the claim is supposed to be. As we process the premises at our disposal we may note either an increase or an attenuation in the strength of the claim.

One mechanism by which claims are attenuated is the reservation. A reservation is an exception to the warrant. In Toulmin's language, it indicates "circumstances in which the general authority of the warrant would have to be set aside."

A reservation is like a disclaimer in an insurance policy. They won't pay off if you destroy something on purpose. The key word you can use to indicate a reservation is "unless."

For example, if a person is making a claim that "you should wear a seatbelt at all times when driving," the warrant might be the general principle that "seatbelts save lives." One who wants to attenuate the claim may make reservations about the warrant, such as "unless you are hit from the side." The reservation itself, of course, is a premise which must be acceptable to the audience.

Reservations frequently have a cumulative effect. It is not uncommon in an audience debate for the first response to a major claim to take the form of a reservation. With respect to the above seatbelt claim, someone in the audience may simply ask, "What about the case of a person who has had a recent surgical operation in the abdomen?" If a reservation is established on such an exception, it may not have much impact, but a whole lot of reservations could weaken the claim to the point of unacceptability. Watch out for the "what abouts."

Reservations face the same standards of verifiability and relevance that data face, so debaters and audience members retain the complex responsibilities of evaluating any argument from many points of view.

SYSTEMIC ARGUMENT

There is some suggestion in what we have been saying and in our use of the Toulmin model that argumentation is exclusively a linear process. Far from it. Almost every effort to construct a proof of a proposition consists of a substantial web of interrelated data, warrants, reservations, and claims.

In a "system" of any kind, the operation of one part may affect another. Thus, if we see a debate case as a system of some sort, we will need to ask what effect a particular piece of data or warrant has upon a multitude of associated and interrelated points. Further, changes in one warrant may affect the applicability and viability of another. If we are debating about a proposal to increase the weight limits on trucks using the interstate highway system, facts having to do with the present condition of some of these interstates may affect the picture of tax rates, of safety features, and even something like national defense or quality of roadbuilding materials. A simple warrant like "increased truck taxes will raise more revenue" would become problematic if in another part of the situation more pipelines became available and economically feasible. There isn't just one conclusion we might draw, but a system which needs to be re-evaluated.

Thus two important final questions we ask when processing the premises we have available are "Where does this fit in?" and "How does this piece of data affect the whole picture?"

Chapter 10

Continuity and Clash

To make a public debate dull and uninteresting takes real effort. By its very nature, debate means conflict and contains the dramatic elements which are inherent in competition of any kind. In audience debating the listeners themselves not only respond but participate and add to the clash of contradictory arguments. Unpredictable and unexpected views may pop up at any moment from among the many individuals who represent multifarious views and interests on the subject, and who cannot conveniently ignore one another. If the topic you are debating has any salience at all, the conflict inherent in audience debate will make for a dynamic and exciting occasion.

Public deliberation also implies a certain amount of control. No matter how dynamic and exciting the contest is, the abstract demands of reasoned discourse as well as the concrete insistence of the concerned persons who are attending the debate will require an orderly procedure of analysis and argument, where evidence and claims are logically linked and where basic issues are dealt with systematically. The meaningful evaluation of significant arguments is an intellectually disciplined endeavor, and a good public debate will stimulate and produce orderly thought. In other words, there'll be method in the madness.

Any particular debate, then, unfolds as a total event with a beginning and an ending, with variety and unity, and with a discernible pattern in which the parts can be seen as put together in a coherent way. Our awareness and use of the explicit techniques of continuity and clash will contribute to reinforcing what is significant, weeding out a lot of the inanities, and producing a worthwhile debate.

THREADS OF CONTINUITY

If a debate is to unfold in a comprehensible way, one thing should lead to another. An advocate of the development of geothermal energy may cite the Raft River pilot plant in Oregon as an example of the economic feasibility of generating electricity from thermal sources. Isolated, this example means little in the debate, but when it is used as a paradigmic example with further explanation or when it is augmented with other examples to produce a generalization, it begins to build a significant theme.

Generally the major threads of continuity in a debate will consist of what the participants consider to be the most vital issues. We keep coming back to these because we sense that the listeners will regard them as important for understanding the question or for making their decisions. An issue may emerge as central in a given debate either because it is insisted upon by one or more of the participants or because a number of speakers refer to it frequently. Debaters who wish to create continuity will give their first attention to the issues which their own study of the subject matter area and their analysis of the audience lead them to see as vital. In like manner, the central value or the central drama referred to in Chapter 6, rather than the central issue, may turn out to provide the most suitable thread of continuity.

The central vital issue (or value or drama) is not the only feature about which the elements of continuity may cluster, though. For instance, you can look for a vivid, typical, or well-known example to which you can relate your arguments. In debates on the subject of limiting press coverage of courtroom trials, the case of Dr. Sam Shepherd frequently becomes the focus of much attention from everyone in the debate. When mercy killing is under consideration, the example of Karen Quinlan is used for similar reasons. In other debates, a less familiar instance having been described by one side may be picked up by the other in order to establish continuity. "Let's just take another look at the snail darter case," they may say.

Not infrequently a striking metaphor will serve as a common thread in a debate. If a team advocating a shift in foreign policy options uses language to the effect that the ship of state is sinking, we can expect to hear much talk in that debate about "reaching port," "plugging leaks," and "man overboard."

Even a simple but memorable phrase will be useful for thematic reverberation. In all kinds of efforts to exert public influence, advocates look for slogans such as "right-to-work" and "truth-in-lending" to identify the causes which they are pushing. In any particular debate event, a group of words as plain as "poor George" or "a simple situation" may provide a central or incidental reference of value if repeated at the right times and with the right inflections. "'Poor George' may not be so bad off," we may be told, and this will form another thread of continuity.

Any of these threads may be managed in four elementary ways: repeating, extending, incorporating, and relating.

Repeating. Any point worth stating is worth repeating. The famous old rule of debate is "Tell 'em what you're going to tell 'em, tell 'em, and tell 'em what you told 'em."

Major contentions especially should be previewed, stated, repeated, and summarized. The very act of reminding the audience what the important points are helps give coherence to the debate.

Reiteration itself has traditionally been a standard form of support in writing and speaking. Let me repeat that. Reiterating itself has traditionally been a standard form of support in writing and speaking. In debate such repetition has the function of signalling that a contention or phrase is of special weight or significance. Insofar as we also respond to what is familiar, it may have persuasive impact as well. Especially for those who are not taking notes, it serves as a reminder of what has already been said.

Especially important in this regard are the final summary speeches when these are called for by the rules, because here each side reinforces important points which they have made and thus they assist in the process of final decision making.

Extending. The process of "extending" an argument, one of the first things a student of debating usually learns, consists of offering additional evidence or additional lines of reasoning to support a point in later speeches after it has once been made in a debate.

Usually the nature of the extension will be determined by the kind of response which has been made by opposing speakers or by the kinds of questions which have been asked. If an opponent denies the qualifications of the source of your evidence, your extension will reinforce those qualifications. If you are accused by an audience member of having made a "hasty generalization" from a single example, your extension will consist of additional examples to support your point. And in cases where listeners express a simple puzzlement about what we mean, we can extend by a plain explanation of the point we made. Our extensions, of course, will often call forth responses from other speakers, leading to further extensions until a decisive answer can be given.

Even if no substantial attack has been made, an important point may be extended in order to keep it in a prominent place among the decision considerations. Although logically a point stands in a debate if it has not been attacked, such an ignored contention may still be reinforced for the listeners with additional evidence and reasoning.

In an audience debate, extension of arguments not only serves the logical function of providing material crucial to the resolution of disputed issues, but also creates necessary strands of continuity which give unity and structure to the event.

Incorporating. As we have noticed before, a basic feature of most formats in audience debate is active participation of a large diversity of individuals. One of the ways we are going to establish continuity in such a setting, then, is to try to incorporate materials which have already been introduced somewhere by other speakers when we are setting forth or reinforcing important contentions. For instance, if the subject is gun control legislation, various participants will probably introduce on one side or the other examples of persons who have accidentally shot members of their own families or perhaps of persons who have successfully defended themselves from attack because they had hand guns. We can use such examples as well as other kinds of evidence and lines of argument set forth by audience members, to support our own cause. The fact that we can make a simple reference to an example everyone has already heard tends to make the debate more cohesive. Making references to other speakers and incorporating their views and personal experiences into our own welds the group into a more integrated decision-making body.

Perceptive participants will be especially alert to "feedback" which indicates that a specific argument, a good example, or a colorful phrase has had a notable impact on the audience, or at least has caught their attention, and will use such materials as building blocks of their own advocacy. We can even incorporate materials introduced by opponents of our position, especially if they are susceptible to such refutational techniques as "turning the tables." Any public debate will profit from alertness on the part of all participants to the mutually accessible discourse which can be incorporated in ensuing arguments to augment its structure and continuity.

Relating. A fourth method of maintaining continuity is to establish the habit of relating any contribution explicitly to the major issues and contentions of the debate. Ask yourself, "Where does the point I am making fit into this debate?"

Any public debate which involves a substantial amount of audience participation will be composed of a great mosaic of "short takes," including relatively brief speeches and comments, questions, and answers to questions. A certain proportion of these contributions will follow an associational "that reminds me" mode of informal conversation or will be idiosyncratic remarks not especially related to anything else at all. However, particularly when you're getting only one chance to speak, you will want to relate your specific questions or opinions to the on-going development of the issues. This is a task which the principal speakers and everyone else in the debate will share. Prefacing your question, answer, or comment with such a phrase as "with reference to the issue of whether the proposed board of control will operate in the public interest" will improve the sense of perspective of all of the participants.

Maintaining unity and continuity in a debate is dependent upon keeping it structured and organized in the face of a wide range of individual viewpoints and lines of argument. The habit of relating all of the points which are made to this structure therefore contributes to sounder decision making.

POINTS OF CLASH

Clash, of course, is vital to debate. The dispute which we establish by setting forth a controvertible proposition and by delegating a defense and an opposition to it, a process which is at the heart of debate, is carried forward by further disagreement at every level of argument. Logically, the clarification and resolution of the differences between the contradictory positions of the two sides depends upon the efforts of all of the participants to locate and specify the points of clash which separate them.

Audiences expect a clash. Among the motives which bring us to a debate may be the desire to see how the conflicting positions compare with one another, to participate ourselves in an attack upon views we deem to be mistaken or in a defense of those which we are committed to, or possibly just to witness a good fight. As an unfolding event, a public debate requires that everyone should be conscious of clash as well as continuity.

Essentially, clash is established whenever there is refutation, and refutation can be applied to almost anything that is said. Refutation is the process of setting forth weaknesses in opposing arguments, either in the strength of the argument itself or in its significance or relevance. The many probes discussed in Chapter 8 provide you with a healthy store of weaknesses in the analysis, evidence, and reasoning used to support a proposition. You may also want to become familiar with descriptions of special methods of refutation, such as dilemmas and *reductio ad absurdum*, which depend upon locating internal inconsistencies in the arguments which have been presented.

Although clash may be established on almost anything, you can't and shouldn't try to refute everything. Establishing the points of clash in a debate involves some stringent selectivity. The major clashes should be reserved for points which you think are very important and which have a substantial bearing on the vital issues. Clash may furthermore take place on points which seem to have had an impact on a number of audience members because the points were especially incisive or colorful. Individual audience members may choose to create clash on a certain matter because they happen to have special knowledge or experience having a direct bearing upon it.

Obviously, you aren't the only one around who is choosing when to have a clash, because your designated opponents and members of the audience are also making their choices, to which you may have to respond. In making these choices, we generally try to avoid the temptation to jump on points which are trivial mistakes on minor facts or simple misstatements. (Even here, this is no set rule, as sometimes trivial errors may be arguably symptomatic, as in a claim that "They don't even know who the Prime Minister of Canada is.") Recalling that there are many debates going on in many minds, we may also discover that some participants make speeches which are too tangential or irrelevant to merit any response at all. In any event, since you can't clash on everything, choose carefully those points of clash which will contribute most to the debate as a whole.

In preparing for public debate, advocates may well spend as much energy studying the "other side" as they do their own in order to choose appropriate points of clash and to be ready for whatever happens. One method is to prepare some of your answers ahead of time, a process which is known in the trade as "blocking," where you develop and organize blocks of material you may want to use for refutational or critical points whenever they come up. Adaptation is vital in a debate, and we always run into some surprises, but clash should be as well prepared for as is the constructive argument supporting our case.

In maintaining continuity and clash, we should remind ourselves, it is necessary to tell people what we're doing. To establish a clash (or to engage in refutation generally), we try to make sure that we explain what point we are clashing with, indicate clearly our objections to it, and then present the impact of our refutation on that point and upon the status of the major issues.

At its most general level, the clash will take place on what in Latin is referred to as the *status*, the point upon which the dispute as a whole rests. The discovery of this point will emerge from a consideration of the affirmative case, the negative response to it, and the agreement of the participants. It most often will be a basic stock issue, such as whether the advantages of the proposal outweigh the disadvantages of it. However, in a debate which gets narrowed down, the status may be, among other possibilities, a field-dependent matter such as what research method is most relevant in a given case. In any event, it is as much a matter of audience perception as of the presumable logic of the positions of the contending parties. And at the more concrete levels, clash will take place on any matter that anyone wants to dispute, ranging from the quality of the logical reasoning being employed to the details of a visual aid map.

Any of the points of clash which have been selected by the participants may be managed in four elementary ways: denying, countering, minimizing, or reframing.

Denying. The most blunt method for establishing clash is to deny outright the truth of what the other side is saying. Show that something they said just isn't so; this is direct refutation.

The denial may be at the analytical level. For instance, we may say that although the affirmative side has described a problem, they have failed even to contend that their proposal would solve it, and thus they have failed to demonstrate that we should adopt that proposal. There is a complete gap in the case they have presented.

The denial may also occur at the evidential level, where we may prove that a fact or statistic which opponents have cited is completely inaccurate, or where the authority they have quoted never said what they attributed to him or her. In fact, their failure to cite any evidence at all for some contention may also be noted in refutation. As we can see, good and careful listening is essential to effective refutation and to see where these gaps appear.

The objective in clash in a debate is to reach a resolution by which one side or the other turns out to be right. That determination, naturally, is made by the audience members. Refutation has been accomplished when a substantial proportion of the audience discounts or discards the argument under attack. Since the eventual outcome depends entirely upon audience assent, any attempt at refutation is itself a line of argument. Even so-called fallacies, conventionally regarded as fatal flaws in the reasoning process, are ultimately mere lines of argument, as is the very claim that the reasoning is fallacious. "Fallacies" have some logical force to them in someone's mind or they would not be uttered in the first place. As an example, a contention that a new set of police regulations caused the crime rate to go down may be dismissed with a *post hoc ergo propter* hoc label, but the audience may still find the argument credible even when it manifests what appears to be a fallacy in informal reasoning.

Even when a complete denial does not carry weight with all of the members of the audience, it remains an effective and dramatic method of establishing clash.

Countering. The process of counter-argument, in contrast with the direct attack upon the truth or validity of what the other side has said, builds a parallel line of argument which leads to a contrary conclusion or presents evidence which contradicts the opponents' facts. This countering procedure also establishes a legitimate clash.

For instance, to go back to the crime rate, debaters recently noted a reduction in the crime rate as reflected in FBI statistics and quoted an authority who claimed that stricter law enforcement had been the cause of the phenomenon. This causal argument was often countered with population statistics which were claimed to show that the decrease was caused by a reduction in the members of the age group who were most likely to commit crimes.

There's nothing wrong with using what are called "counter-warrants" in audience debates. To do this, a debater simply prepares constructive lines of argument which come to a different conclusion than the one which has been adduced by the opposition. Such arguments can be prepared ahead of time. The main danger in this and other types of pre-prepared counter-argument is that the parallel cases may not clash directly enough, like ships that pass in the night, and that the participants will not then work hard enough to resolve the issues.

You may be tempted to present a "counterplan," a somewhat riskier business. A counterplan is a new proposal designed to accomplish what has been claimed for the propositional plan and to do it better. The audience in this case gets to compare the desirability of what are in effect two different proposals. Sometimes, audiences even explicitly demand that anyone attacking a given plan come up with one of his or her own. The risk here comes from unduly complicating the debate and from making the clash less explicit.

If the point of the clash can be kept in focus, counter-argument should be a standard part of the audience debater's repertoire.

Minimizing. Almost any point which an opposing speaker will make has some truth to it. A third way of managing clash is to take that fact into account by insisting that this point, no matter how "true," is actually not very important and should not weight heavily in anyone's decision regarding the proposition. The problem they have described is hardly a big problem, or the disadvantage they have claimed is not a powerful one. We must minimize what they have to say by downplaying its significance.

In minimizing (or maximizing, for that matter), you try to consider two kinds of significance, quantitative and qualitative. Quantitative significance takes a statistical form, so that we can minimize the impact of a claim by saying that not very many lives are at stake or not much money would be saved. Using formal statistical procedures and norms, we can demonstrate that certain claimed correlations and differences are not really significant. Qualitative significance brings to bear important unquantifiable values such as human dignity, social cohesion, or beauty. Human life is generally regarded as so valuable that to save even a few lives may be judged to be significant. On the other hand, millions of people may be afflicted with broken finger nails (quantitatively impressive), but qualitatively the problem isn't worth bothering about and thus may easily be minimized.

Clashes on the basis of significance usually have some kind of comparison at their base. We minimize by making comparisons. In defense of nuclear power plants, speakers may say that individuals get more dangerous radiation from wearing tight underwear than from such plants, or that dangers from other power sources such as coal mines are much greater.

When the clash over significance becomes central to a given debate, the process of minimizing becomes very important. Don't minimize minimizing. Audiences are not likely to support action on a matter which they are convinced doesn't matter very much.

Reframing. One other important method of establishing clash in a debate is to lead the audience to put the matter into a different frame of reference by restructuring the argument or reinterpreting its meaning. "Let's try to look at in this way," would be the key line.

Ambitiously, we can reframe the whole case. For instance, a bureaucracy which has been pictured as inefficient and lacking in unity may be seen, with the same evidence, as admirably flexible and able to meet the variegated needs of those it serves. We change the picture by introducing the new values of flexibility and responsiveness.

"Turning the tables" is a well-known method of refutation which rests upon the principle of reframing the argument. When the claim is made that building a new bridge will have the advantage of stimulating industrial development on the West Mesa, the "turnaround" may be that industrial development there would be a bad thing rather than a good one.

The clash in these cases then turns upon the issue of "how should we look at this question?"

QUESTIONS AND ANSWERS

Because direct involvement from as many of the participants as possible is an aim of most public debate, you're going to get lots of questions and answers in these events. The format will normally encourage them, whether during cross-examination periods among the principal speakers, as periods designated for questions from the audience, as handled by a delegated panel of respondents, as taken in written form from the listeners, or as completely incidental features of the open forum period. Questions perform the important functions of showing what audience members are worried about and giving them a chance to find out what they need to know in order to make decisions.

Hazards arise from the fact that questions and answers often are not imbedded in continuous discourse where their relevance can be made readily apparent. In order to maintain a coherent pattern of continuity and clash, therefore, we have to be especially conscious of the necessity of formulating answers in constructive ways.

For instance, in asking a question, particularly when it does not arise sequentially from a question or answer preceding it, speakers need to provide a context sufficient to show where it fits in. Audience members can't always get recognition from the chairperson the exact moment when their questions might be most appropriate. They might not even think of them at that moment. In asking the question, then, one might say something like, "I want to go back to the contention about thermal pollution and ask a question about how it occurs."

Just as important is to provide a meaningful "wrapping" to the answers we give to the questions that are asked. While at times listeners will welcome a simple yes or no, ordinarily they need to be told what effect the respondent thinks the answer will have. Especially in the case of "hostile" questions, the respondent will want to turn the attention of the audience to the central claim from which it grew. You try to bounce back to an upright position, like one of those toy clowns with a weighted base.

The question and answer process is a fertile ground for the development of lucid continuity and clash in a debate as long as the participants keep the whole debate in mind and recognize the function of what they are doing.

TAKING NOTES

To manage all of this continuity and clash in a debate requires not only good listening and speedy responses, but also efficient note-taking. We have to find a way to get this stuff down in a form where we can work with it.

The customary method for taking debate notes is called "keeping a flow." Every debater should know how to do it. A flow consists of a record of the remarks of each speaker put down in columns on a large pad (such as a legal pad) with one column allotted to each speech. Keeping a flow allows any participant to follow the progress of each individual argument as the various speakers deal with it.

In an audience debate, however, you can't do it quite that way. For one thing, there are usually too many different speaker. Also, most of those speakers are not themselves keeping a flow, nor can they get themselves recognized for speeches at exactly the time most appropriate for the point they are making.

Keeping in mind that our main goal is keeping track of emerging threads of continuity and important points of clash, we need to take a functional approach with regard to taking notes. One helpful procedure is to limit your columns to two, an affirmative and a negative, with perhaps a separate card or piece of paper on which to outline remarks you expect to make yourself. The important thing is to develop headings, including the contentions with which you began the debate, so that remarks and questions, no matter at what point in time they may have been introduced, may be clustered with other similar points that have been made. This procedure may also allow you to "pull' evidence from your research material and indicate where it might be used. All of your notes are designed for the purpose of allowing you to help the audience make a rational decision. The debate itself is not what is in your notes in writing, but what is going on in people's minds. You don't pay attention only to the organized speeches of the principal speakers, but to every remark which indicates what the audience is concerned about.

Most members of the audience do not try to keep notes on the debate, but there's no law against it. If you, as a listener, want to keep a flow of some sort in order to make a better decision or to put yourself into a position to ask sharper questions or add a better point to the debate, then in this role also you can work on what is the best form of note-taking for you.

CONCLUDING SPEECHES

In most formats for audience debating, another feature is a time period set aside for one or more representatives of each side to present "concluding speeches."

Any person designated to give a concluding speech should feel an obligation to set forth the best possible selection of arguments which have emerged favoring the side he or she is representing. Although in audience debate there are no formal rules against adding new arguments this late in the debate, the best procedure is to review what is important and to remind the audience what has been said about it. In effect this will be a selective summary.

Among the first things to consider in doing this speech would be the significant issues which have come out. Presumably these have formed part of the fabric of the continuity in the debate and have been the scene for the important clashes. Pick out the main points and the central issues, demonstrating the superiority of your position regarding them. Also worth reminding people about are the more colorful or memorable examples and metaphors which have been used on your side.

Selectivity is especially important. You can never cover everything that has been said, and you don't have to. You're trying to remind the audience of what is salient. Dropping some arguments is necessary, and talking real fast is counter-productive.

A public debate is a thinking match, with everyone directly participating in the thinking. It is nothing like a boxing match, where spectators simply cheer for their favorites and collect their bets. One standard feature of a concluding speech is a reminder to the audience that they are voting on the question at hand, not on which team did the better job of debating. They are to vote on what they actually believe, and this should be part of the final appeal.

Since debate is not a spectator sport, the more team play you can demonstrate among all the players on your side the better. The concluding speech should incorporate items from many members of the audience and should give the impression that the "we" of the affirmative or negative includes not just the teams on the platform but a sizable segment of the audience.

The concluding speeches, then, are directly related to the vote which will ordinarily follow, and should assist everyone in making the vote an intelligent one.

Chapter 11

Facilitating Communication

No argument may be regarded as established if it has not been heard and understood by listeners. Speakers and audience members alike share a responsibility for maintaining the kind of communicative atmosphere which will make rational evaluation of propositions possible.

Public argument is manifestly a social enterprise. Since it involves people and has consensual judgment as its ultimate objective, this form of decision-making is highly dependent upon effective processes of communication. You have to communicate well to debate well.

Since throughout this book we have been using relatively formal, face-to-face audience debate as our primary exemplar of public argument, we will continue in this chapter to deal explicitly with communication which is oral. However, it should be remembered that effective communication remains central not only to oral argument, but to writing and any other medium in which argument is conducted.

We'll define communication as the mutual understanding of the meaning of symbolic messages. If the understanding is not mutual, you don't have communication. For instance, suppose that someone utters the following message: "At the   present rate of CFC production, the ozone layer will be reduced by 10 percent in the next 50 years." If those who hear it don't know what CFC or an ozone layer is, then shared meanings are at a minimum.   The communication is poor and you haven't proved anything. You have some explaining to do.

Making your meanings clear does not mean talking baby-talk, though. In most instances when you are debating about pollution, your listeners will know perfectly well what CFC and the ozone layer are, and you can go ahead with your reasoning without further explanation. That's good communication.

Effective communication is generally dependent upon a process known as "feedback," which is the adjustment of messages to the responses of receivers. For the feedback process to work, speakers and audience members alike will continually monitor what's going on to see whether they should be making any adjustments in what they are saying or in their listening. As we've all heard, communication is a two-way street. Sometimes the feedback will consist of explicit statements such as "I don't understand that," or "you don't seem to get what I'm trying to say." Frequently the process is more subtle and operates through nonverbal channels. In any event, it makes no sense for a speaker to plow ahead with a line of argument, no matter how brilliant, if no one is listening or if the audience is confused about what the person is saying. It does make sense to keep the audience responses in mind at all times and to watch for signs of feedback.

When you stop to think about it, all of the aspects of debate we've been considering depend on communication. For instance, to debate at all we have to have a mutual understanding of what a proposition means. The premises we use have to be mutually understood and ultimately agreed upon. A shared agreement about such matters as issues, warrants, and other elements is necessary for good continuity and clash in a debate. In other words, choosing lines of argument which will make sense to listeners is the most important part of the communication process.

When we look at communication in terms of classical Greek and Roman rhetoric, we are usually told about its five canons, namely: (1)

invention, (2) arrangement, (3) style, (4) delivery, and (5) memory. The term "invention" refers to the discovery and choice of appropriate logical arguments and other persuasive appeals. Invention is what we have been considering in the preceding chapters and we should keep that most important aspect of rhetoric in mind as we now look at the other canons, namely, the organization of ideas (arrangement), verbal communication (style), and nonverbal communication (delivery). We'll forget memory, but will conclude discussion of the matter of facilitating communication by looking at the ways in which debate can be maintained as a humane and ethical endeavor.

THE ORGANIZATION OF IDEAS

Lucid organization of our ideas is one important way to facilitate communication in a public argumentation. The processes of structuring arguments and using transitions assist the audience to comprehend relationships among those arguments and to remember them as decisions are being formulated in their minds.

In organizing ideas for presentation, speakers and writers will be governed to some extent by formal logical expectations, the substantive nature of the subject-matter field, and the knowledge and expertise of the audience. Matters such as the definition of terms logically come earlier in a presentation. The "stock issues" described in Chapter 6 may guide organization as well as analysis. Propositions concerning disparate fields in science or religion may carry their own structural expectations.

In any event, though, the audience will always be a factor.

To create identification with a particular group, for instance, it may be well to organize your material in a manner which moves from the known to the unknown or from agreed upon premises to premises less agreed upon. An audience which is familiar with and favorable to zoning regulations on a local level may respond to a reinforcement of those attitudes before the speaker moves on to apply the same principles to national land use legislation. Thus the "plan" might be defended first. In another case, such as health care, it may be that the audience is most cognizant of deficiencies in the present system, which would for purposes of identification as well as logical structure be placed first in a presentation. You try to follow their line of thinking.

Even formal structure creates identification, according to rhetorician Kenneth Burke.

A familiar problem-solution structure may prove most desirable because in our culture people are used to it and will frequently be psychologically "demanding" a solution contention even before the problem is completely demonstrated. Burke at another place describes form as "the arousing and fulfillment of desires." You can lead listeners to expect a certain kind of development and they will themselves participate in that development as you go along.

It is easiest to organize a case when you are one of the principal speakers at the beginning of a debate, of course. However, if we are members of the audience we will also have the option of accepting a structure we hear set forth or of making the attempt to structure these arguments for ourselves. A commonly accepted organization developing around the emerging issues in a debate is not unusual, where everyone takes part in the structuring process.

Argumentation is reasoned discourse, so when you are outlining it on paper you normally will try to follow a didactic form in which any subordinate point you have is a reason for accepting the point to which it is subordinate. A parallel point will be given coordinate status in the outline. For example:

I.   State lotteries tend to hurt lower income groups
    A.   They take the form of regressive taxation
        1.   Lower income groups tend to spend a higher proportion of their pay on them
            a.   Example of Joe Blow
            b.   Statistic from university study
            c.   You know richer people don't participate
    B.   Low income individuals take money from necessities to spend on lottery tickets
        1.   They will spend less on food and clothing
            a.   Newspaper survey
            b.   Interviews with ticket buyers

The major points on such an outline are main contentions and the most subordinate points are the accepted premises. This structure is normally reflected in oral presentation as well, as it makes all arguments more understandable and "negotiable." We all know where we stand and can effectively subject the argumentation to careful scrutiny.

Transitions and summaries are especially functional in audience situations. "Signposting" is a popular term for the process of using transitions as guides or warnings. A signpost, which may be a simple phrase such as "secondly," tells a listener to be ready for another point and to become aware of its relationship to preceding arguments. Such signposts must be fully stated enough to be clear. Often "secondly" is not sufficient and the situation calls for something like this: "This plan is practical. We have shown that our proposed system has worked in other countries. Now let's see that we have the resources and trained manpower to make it work here."

As has been suggested, organizational structure develops and changes during the course of any given debate. Everyone involved uses a tentative structure as a map in which to tuck points as they are made. The major points presented in speeches later in the encounter and the order in which they are placed will depend upon what opposing advocates have said and what issues have emerged as apparent decision points for members of the audience. The whole aim is clear communication.

THE WORDS WE USE

The words we choose to use in a debate make a difference in the listener's understanding and reception of what we have to say. The choice and arrangement of words are the essential elements of "style" in speaking. We can talk in many different ways.

Although the complexities of style are a factor in every kind of written and spoken communication, certain stylistic tensions are inherent in public argument. To these a debater should give some conscious attention.

Specialized vs. Common Language. We already noted that terms such as CFC and ozone layer may cause difficulties in communication if they are not comprehended by the listeners. The choice a speaker faces in this case is whether to use the specialized vocabulary applicable to the subject area being debated or to use more common terminology which may make the argument less precise and efficient. What technical terms will this audience understand? Which ones are important enough to require explanation if listeners don't understand them?

Sticking to a common and generally recognized vocabulary has the advantage of making your arguments accessible to almost everyone and allows for the kind of full participation which is desirable in public debate.

However, with any topic which has gained much public attention some of the specialized vocabulary will have become commonly known, as with "O-Rings" in space technology or "false positives" in drug testing topics. Most of the time we may comfortably use such terms.

And in some cases the audience will be very well informed about the topic and indeed may comprehend the relevant terminology as well as we do. Debates, it might be noted, tend to attract persons who know something about the topic already. As usual, careful audience analysis becomes very useful, even in the matter of vocabulary in a debate. We don't want to underuse or overuse specialized language.

What is true of special vocabularies of a topic is also true of the jargon of logic and academic debate. Some technical terms we might use in a classroom, such as "affirming the consequent" or "flow it across" might simply impede understanding on an ordinary public occasion, but when the audience understands technical meanings of terms such as "inherency," the debate may possibly be improved by using them.

Formal vs. Informal Style. Style may be classified into a broad continuum ranging from the most informal and colloquial to the extremely formal and dignified.

In public argument, on the one hand the formal nature of argumentation and the complexity of many of the arguments we employ press us in the direction of a formal language use, with longer and more complex sentences. On the other hand, the necessity for flexibility and adaptability leads discourse in the informal and conversational direction, with shorter sentences and more colloquial language.

One explicit choice we face is whether to write out and read what we have to say or to present our ideas extemporaneously from notes. Experience suggests that the advantages lie with extemporaneous delivery and a conversational style. Most audiences respond more actively to conversational language and the informal style generally allows for more adaptability and response to feedback in the speaking situation. In other words, there's better communication.

Clarity vs. Interest. While being clear and being interesting may often enough go hand in hand, a certain tension may also exist between these goals.

To be clear usually calls for precision in language, explicit transitional statements, and frequent repetition. To be interesting means using unusual and surprising language along with figurative devices such as including irony, hyperbole, and rhetorical questions. If the audience does not catch on to the irony, there will be a communication failure. Where the language seems dull, there may be boredom and inattention.

Wherever this tension exists, probably clarity is the first criterion and interest the second. Certainly the contentions which form the basis of an argument should be formulated with some precision. To contend that "the situation in Bosnia is not all that great" does not provide a sufficient basis for rational evaluation. Still, repartee and imagination and humor are among the attractive elements of an audience debate. You have to admit that hyperbole is the greatest thing in the world.

The primary aim of stylistic choice is to enhance communication, the way the symbols are understood. Whenever we change our wording, we change the argument to a degree. Therefore, the wording we employ will always affect the meaning of the argumentation in a debate. We always try to choose the wording which will best create an understanding between ourselves and our listeners.

NONVERBAL COMMUNICATION

Many of the meanings generated in an audience debate are derived from nonverbal visual and vocal symbols. Speakers show what they mean and listeners figure out what those meanings are partly on the basis of gestures and vocal inflections.

We could continue to refer to this nonverbal behavior as delivery, but the term delivery might suggest somehow that we are wrapping words in a package and handing them to someone else. Since the nonverbal behaviors are usually part of the meaning rather than separate from it, we can best think of this symbolic activity as a special kind of communication Thus, the voice augments verbal meaning and in effect sometimes adds ideas of its own.

Among other uses, speakers will employ vocal elements and visual symbols (physical activity and visual aids) to clarify what they mean, to emphasize and reinforce important points, and even to replace words in making arguments.

Using Your Voice

Nonverbal means "other than words." Therefore, the ways speakers use their voices in conjunction with words also contribute to the facilitation of communication in an audience debate. It's not just that you have to talk loudly enough to be heard, but also to give clues to listeners as to what you mean.

The main elements a speaker may want to think about when using his or her voice are (1) loudness, (2) pitch, (3) time, (4) quality, (5) articulation, and (6) pronunciation. Infinite variations are available with respect to each of these elements. "Time," for instance, encompasses not only the general rate at which a person speaks, but also speeding up or slowing down at various points, pauses of different lengths, and stretching out or clipping off words. "Pitch" includes variations within sentences and even within syllables (inflections), as well as how high or low a person's voice habitually is.

The Uses of Voice. Yes, you do have to talk loudly enough. The first necessity of vocal usage is to make sure that the words are heard and absorbed by the audience. A speaker should articulate clearly, project vocally to the whole audience, and pause often enough to allow ideas to sink in.

But, as suggested earlier, vocal cues add meanings of their own. An upward inflection converts a declarative statement into a question. Increased vocal force or a marked pitch change on a word gives it special emphasis within a sentence. Try it out. See whether you can change the meaning of this sentence by altering your vocal emphasis or inflections.

A person's vocal cues may also indicate how the listeners are supposed to "take" a certain passage. A sentence may be employed ironically, and the voice will indicate that "I don't mean this at all." Are we supposed to regard a point as very important or as rather subordinate and incidental? The voice may tell us. And vocally expressed emotional intonations, as of anger or fear, are not irrelevant to the argumentative process.

The listener has some obligation to read these nonverbal vocal cues, sometimes to be on guard against them, but more frequently to pick up the full flavor of the arguments being communicated and thus make a better decision. An audience member may legitimately discount evidence which is uttered with apparent hesitancy. (Do you agree with that?) As a listener, one may also want to work on ways of responding to arguments which are embedded in nonverbal vocal behaviors.

What does a debater do, then? Probably no one will want to practice particular vocal expressions. Still, to expand one's vocal range and repertoire may be useful. Certainly to be fully responsive to what one is saying will be reflected to some extent in one's voice. And listening to other speakers and engaging in criticism of the vocal elements of communication would also no doubt be helpful.

Some Hazards. Rate of speaking may be the most difficult vocal element for a debater to utilize properly. Most of the pressures of debate, especially set time limits, tend to push a person in the direction of speaking very rapidly. Thus the "motormouth." Although research has consistently demonstrated that listeners can comprehend messages transmitted at far faster rates than any speaker is likely to use, rapid-fire presentation is not necessarily a good idea for most audiences. It tends to be distracting and call attention to itself and, although comprehensible, may not allow for thought and deliberation about the points being made.

Other vocal elements also may be used in the light of the audience response to a message. Shouting, for instance, is more likely to suggest insecurity than to provide appropriate emphasis. A flat monotone may indicate that the message is not important.

Oral reading in a debate also requires special attention. In strict parliamentary procedure, such reading is not allowed at all except by permission of the assembly. Reading of quotations for evidence is not necessarily objectionable for most audiences, however, as long as the reading is communicative. To read well means to keep in mind the objective of establishing the point or the evidence with listeners, so appropriate vocal variety, rate of reading, and awareness of feedback response are essential.

Physical Activity

Do you think it is possible to prove or disprove a contention with a mere facial expression? On one campus where the merits of the fraternity and sorority system were the subject of a public debate, an advocate of the system claimed that "there isn't any 'hazing' by fraternities and sororities any more." The nonverbal reply from a spokesman for the other side was a facial expression of incredulity. This expression generated images and assumptions in the minds of audience members much as if the person had made a verbal contention to the effect that "we contend, on the contrary, that a substantial amount of hazing does indeed still go on." An incident such as this might be referred to as "argument through facial expression," a physical movement functioning as a logical statement.

We all read some kind of meaning into the physical activity of other individuals as we talk or listen to them during a debate. The "body language" we observe consists of facial expression, eye contact, gestures, movement, posture, and general personal appearance. Shrugging the shoulders, raising the eyebrows, or striding vigorously across the platform are among the many actions providing clues to a communicator's ideas and intentions.

The Uses of Body Language. The construction of nonverbal contentions is not the primary use of physical action in communication, though. The direct substitution of nonverbal symbols for words, or "emblems" such as nodding yes or no, is secondary to the utilization of physical activity as a kind of paralanguage, clarifying and emphasizing what the words themselves are saying.

For clarification, a speaker may use movement or facial expression to indicate transitions or whether a point should be taken ironically or seriously. For emphasis, audiences easily recognize vigorous gestures and head nodding as augmenting the importance of a point being made or even a particular word or phrase.

Receivers also attribute credibility to speakers partially on the basis or personal appearance and "dynamism." They may assume that a person who takes care of his or her appearance is also careful with evidence. However, a person who is "too careful" may suggest someone who needs to be watched. It's a tricky business.

Furthermore, physical communication such as facial response is the most easily available means of feedback for all members of an audience, whether they ever speak or not.

Then what are YOU supposed to do? We would not especially recommend practicing gestures ahead of time, but experience and criticism may make a person's physical activity increasingly more appropriate and effective. So pay some attention to what you do and to what other people do in a debate.

Some Hazards. Physical activity and its interpretation bring some characteristic hazards to both the senders and receivers of communication.

For speakers, too much distracting action (or lack of action) may interfere with the argumentative process. Another thing to be wary of is getting in a rut physically and repeating the same motions too often. Some debaters go into a kind of "dance" as they get absorbed in their notes or their line of thought rather than communication with the audience.

For listeners, the most difficult job is giving the right amount of attention to the physical activity we observe. We may be over-impressed, or we may completely ignore relevant cues. Some people (and you may want to agree with them) would say not to pay any attention at all to such matters of "delivery" because they will distract you from the "argument" in the debate. That's an extreme position, but it might make an interesting topic for a debate some time. Meanwhile, keep your eyes open.

Chapter 12

Evaluation and Decisions

"But who won?" Debate does, after all, have competitive features, so "Who won?" is a natural question for audiences to ask.

Still, as we have noted previously, public debate is not a spectator sport. Most of the time the ultimate judgment of the debate is based upon which side of the resolution seems reasonable to people rather than upon the comparative skills of the advocates. The question of "Who won?" becomes "Which position on the proposition gains the adherence of the audience?"

To some extent the fate of a speaker and a given substantive position are intertwined in the assumptions of public deliberation. Speakers are normally advocating positions to which they are personally committed. If you as an individual are a dedicated partisan of, say, the accelerated development of solar energy, you will probably want the solar energy position to prevail and will feel personally disappointed if it does not win the vote. The substantive vote takes on some of the characteristics of a critical decision.

Besides, there is another assumption in the rationale of audience debate which runs counter to the equation of the final vote in a given situation with the judgment of superiority in debating skills. That is the fact that no given debate exists as an isolated event, such as perhaps a jury trial is conceived to be, but is rather one event in a general public consideration of the issue at hand. Participants are encouraged to use all that they know and feel in making their judgments, whether these factors are a part of the immediate debate or not. Although in a good debate the important evidence and values influencing decisions would normally be brought out into the open, there are and should be influences beyond the control of the speakers. Furthermore, individual value systems may well vary so much among the audience members that even with the most sensitive adaptation no team can assure itself of the ultimate vote.

Although the question of winning and losing is a complex one in public debating, there are indeed some appropriate and helpful procedures for evaluating various aspects of the activity. First and foremost are the considerations which might govern a vote on the merits of the resolution. In other words, at this point you as an audience member would begin to think like a judge, not like an advocate. How do you decide for yourself which position you should give your assent to? How do you decide how to vote? In connection with the determination of such assent, what procedures are available for determining what the audience position actually is? How do you conduct a vote?

Secondly, while our primary concern is always going to be the attitudes of the audience on the subject matter, there may well be times when, for various reasons, we will want to answer the question of "Which team did the better job of debating?" Especially in an educational setting, debate is sometimes looked upon as a contest in personal debating skills, and when such contests are conducted in front of an audience there are still ways of determining who won this contest of skills, so we'll look briefly at these.

Finally, we may well be concerned with evaluating not just the individual debate, but the whole debate program. We need to know how the debating we are doing is perceived by the public and how it may be improved.

WHICH SIDE ARE YOU ON?

Somewhere along the line you have to decide where you stand

with regard to the proposition you are debating. Whether you are one of the relatively committed advocates from the very beginning or you are an undecided audience member trying to form a tentative opinion, you have to figure things out for yourself. You decide which side to support and ultimately which side to vote for. It all comes down to you as an individual.

How do you evaluate the available arguments and decide which side is right for you?

Needless to say, there is no set formula for making rational human decisions. Everything we have said in the previous chapters about analysis, premises, clash, etc., may well apply not only to the public process of debate but also to your individual thinking about it. You are trying to be rational in your decision making. You will therefore attempt to apply standards of argumentation in the most objective and systematic way that you can.

Suppose, then, that you are an audience member who has been listening to a debate. What do you think about?

First of all, you will listen carefully and be as objective as you can. The whole purpose of the debate is to help us think through what we believe. Careful attention to what is said, even the remarks you may look upon as stupid or ill-informed, will give you a wider range of reasons to consider in making your decision. Complete objectivity is impossible to come by, but being open-minded will help you to consider or re-evaluate ideas which may not coincide with your predisposed notions. You can try to see a point from the other person's point of view, since there may be more value to it for you than you had originally thought. Objective listening is your first effort.

Then, as you are thinking about how you are going to vote, try to determine what that vote actually means to you. What does it mean to give your assent to the proposition? Remember that the decision you make will be a tentative one. The first thing that your vote means is that this is the position to which you adhere at this point in time. You can change your mind later. In deciding what the vote means, you also have to determine what the proposition means to you. Quite possibly several interpretations of it have been presented during the debate. Try to think, "What would this proposal mean to

other people if I told them I subscribed to it?" What does your
common sense tell you that it means? That is what you are voting
for. At times it may also be suggested that the public vote will have
repercussions on opinions. In other words, you may need to think of
what impact the very fact of a vote will have. The main thing,
though, is to vote your conscience in accordance with what the
proposition means to you.

You will recall that earlier we said that rational audiences
determine their adherence to a proposition in accordance with what
they think the major issues are. This procedure should therefore be
important to you as an individual member of the audience, of course.
Ask yourself the same question which various speakers have no
doubt asked, "What are the major issues in this debate?" The clash
which has taken place with regard to these major issues will help you
to decide who is right on each of the issues, and thus which position
has the most strength and merits your support. Sometimes a debate
will, in your mind, come down to a single issue. If, for instance, the
plan will simply cost too much, you may not want to support it no
matter how otherwise desirable you think it may be. Or if the
proposal is completely immoral in your view, the other issues may
fade into insignificance to you.

While you are making subdecisions with respect to the important
issues, you have also been "weighing the evidence" which has been
presented during the debate. You have evaluated the facts and
expert opinions that have been offered by advocates of the two sides.
You also, of course, have added in what you know from past
experience, even if no one (including yourself) has actually said it
during the debate. In weighing the evidence, you will furthermore
give substantial consideration to the important values which you
hold. Debate is not just a matter of facts, but of values as well. It
may be that you will find that this process of the intellectual
weighing of the premises will give you an overall decision which will
be more convincing to you than more analytical procedures. Use
whatever there is to use in making your own personal and rational
decision.

It will be useful as you are thinking about the vote you will cast
to go over the actual clash which has taken place on various points.

Where there have been explicit contradictory contentions, try to figure out which side is most nearly right about them. During the debate, naturally, you have had an opportunity to clarify some of these points for yourself. For example, when you have needed further facts or reasoning, you have been able to ask somebody for these facts or reasons. If an argument has seemed particularly strong to you, you have been able to offer it to the other members of the audience and, in effect, test it. You could see what objections might be raised to it. The clash points in a public debate provide opportunities for clarifying your thought and coming to a reasonable conclusion.

Finally, review the whole debate. Add to the arguments you have heard the other thoughts you have had during the debate. Make sure you have thought of everything and that you have listened as objectively as possible. Your final judgment will be a holistic one, based on a total view of the whole proposition. You will vote for the side which, at this moment, makes the most sense to you.

EVALUATING THE QUALITY OF THE DEBATING

Most of the readers of this material are involved in educational endeavors of some kind. You are a student of public debating as well as a participant in it. Therefore, in keeping with educational tradition, you want to know how competent you yourself have become or you want to make judgments as to how competent your students or colleagues in debate are. How do you judge the quality of the debating which your class or organization is conducting?

At this point you will change hats, so to speak, and become a critic and an educator rather than a debater or an audience member. While any discourse will no doubt have an effect upon your opinion, you now become less concerned with whether you personally agree with what is being said and more concerned with how to improve the quality of the argumentation that is addressed to you. You even apply some of the standards which judges of contest or tournament debating might apply.

The judgments developed for your critique must, of course, be applied from the standpoint of the audience where the debate is taking place or, in the case of a "practice" debate, of an assumed audience.

Those who attempt to evaluate the quality of the debating process in a given instance tend to combine in varying degrees two different approaches, an "issues" approach and a "criteria" approach.

In critiquing a debate from an "issues" standpoint, you try to follow the logic of the arguments as they develop. You look at the issues as they emerge and evaluate the adequacy of the support which is provided by the speakers for these issues. In doing this you will probably take a "flow," or set of notes by which you can keep track of the contentions advanced by the two sides. As the debate ends, you can judge the adequacy of the support which has been adduced for each of the contentions and thus decide the status of the argument with regard to each issue.

Certain kinds of questions may be kept in mind as you follow the clash or arguments in the debate you are evaluating.

(1) Are the issues which have been selected for discussion clearly formulated and appropriate for this topic and this audience?

(2) Do the contentions set forth by each side clearly reflect their position with respect to these issues? Are the contentions solidly supported by reasoning and evidence which would be acceptable to the audience they are facing?

(3) Have well-supported "answers" been provided to points made by the other side and to the objections which have been raised to their own contentions? Has the "clash" been thorough and persistent? Have important points been unfortunately dropped?

One side or the other may be said to have "won" an issue if the support they have provided for it is superior to that provided in opposition to it and if important objections to it have been adequately answered. Your evaluation of the debate will point out such matters as the strongly supported points which are to be commended and the possibilities for better support or more thorough refutation with respect to those which have not been adequately presented.

It might be remembered that in a public debate with audience participation, many points of view and many levels of argumentation are to be expected. Some of the lines of argument are going to be difficult to follow and consistency cannot always be maintained. In other words, contradictory contentions may be presented even by those purporting to be on the same side of the resolution, and part of your job as a critic may be to point out any problems which this fact may cause.

Now suppose we decide to look at the debate in the light of a set of argumentation "criteria." We do not suddenly start ignoring the issues, but we evaluate in terms of certain standards for audience debate. These standards might include such matters as analysis, evidence, reasoning, refutation, delivery, organization, audience adaptation, and even humor. Appropriate sets of questions might look something like this.

(1) Are the issues which have been selected for development clearly formulated and appropriate for the topic and the audience? (Sound familiar?)

(2) Are the contentions which are set forth well supported with sound and well-documented evidence which is acceptable to this audience?

(3) Is there adequate refutation and clash? Are the significant points raised by the other side answered clearly and thoroughly?

(4) Do the speakers word their arguments in a style which is clear to the listeners and present them with a delivery which clarifies and enhances them, making thoughtful evaluation possible?

(5) Do the speakers adapt to the specific concerns of the audience as expressed in their questions and contributions? Is the debate addressed to this particular set of listeners?

Critics using the criteria approach may even employ a point scale in which they give, say, 1-5 points for each criterion to reflect their evaluations of each aspect of the debate. In any event, questions such as these will provide a basis for individual comments and suggestions for improvement.

The whole point of such criticism and evaluation is to make the debate a better one and to make rational decision-making based upon a substantial consideration of the important issues more possible for the listeners.

WINNING AND LOSING

Naturally enough, people who look upon debate as a contest of personal skills sometimes want to know which team "won." They want to be told which team did the better debating, no matter whom the audience agreed with. There are times when advocates defend very skillfully a position which is not acceptable to a given set of listeners, and occasionally a team debates pathetically even though their position is a popular one.

The idea that the quality of an argument can be judged more or less independently of the opinions of a real audience is central to contest or tournament debating, for instance. A win or loss decision at a debate tournament is determined by a judge trained to consider, so far as possible, only the argumentation presented in the debate by one group of debaters. This is the situation where the debate is a contest of argumentative skill. This activity, we might add, is frequently challenging, enjoyable, and even beneficial, and such demonstrations of mental skill have been an important part of the educational scene for centuries.

This kind of matching of wits may, of course, take place in front of an audience. The audience may even sit passively as spectators and make what they will of the occasion, while one or more expert judges determine who, in their opinion, "won" the debate and announce their decision to the listeners. The audience can then cheer the winners, if they wish. Such an exhibition is not what we have in mind when we talk about audience debating, but the listeners present may still form their own opinions and respond in their minds to the arguments being presented.

Expert judges in a contest mode who are evaluating the comparative skills of two debating teams, while they will normally follow the basic evaluational methods described in the last section, may also be instructed to take into consideration the potential needs and expectations of audiences. An "issues" judge, for example, might be willing to relate the issues being considered in a given debate and the evidence and reasoning used to support contentions in it to the general public debate taking place in society at the time and to the expectations and standards normally applied by knowledgeable citizens. He or she may give credit to "sensible" arguments and penalize ones which can be recognized as outlandish.

If the judge bases his or her decision on a set of established "criteria," then these criteria may also be adjusted in ways which we suggested in the last section. "Audience adaptation" may, indeed, be one of the criteria applied in the judgment. Some of the ballots prepared for tournament debating in the Cross Examination Debate Association (CEDA) follow this principle, so we suggest getting hold of such a ballot.

Now if you don't bring in expert judges to judge your debate, there is another way to decide which team was best. Use "inexpert" judges, namely the members of the audience. Take a vote at the end of the debate, but instead of asking the listeners which side they agree with, you can ask them which team did the better job of debating. (You can also take two votes, one of each kind, if you want to.) The audience members would then presumably apply the kinds of standards suggested in the previous section, even though they aren't trained experts, in casting their votes. The team with the most votes from the audience wins the debate.

There is an even more interesting way to determine which team did the better debating. This is a more or less unobtrusive measure of the change of audience opinions, and it uses what is called a "shift-of-opinion" ballot. With a shift-of-opinion ballot, the audience members actually vote according to their beliefs. In this case, however, they are asked to express their opinions both before and after the debate. The team which wins is the one which "sways" the most opinions in the audience. Even though most members of an audience agree with the affirmative side, for instance, more persons may have shifted in the direction of the negative during the debate than the other way around. Thus the negative speakers may have been the most influential in their argumentation.

Although the fundamental purpose of public debating is to assist concerned persons in making rational decisions about significant public problems, there is an inherent "game" element in the format of debate. We need not completely ignore the fact that listeners may evaluate the quality of debating skill as well as the weight of the arguments being presented to them. Therefore, you can consider whether decisions of this kind will augment or detract from what you are trying to do.

YOUR WHOLE PROGRAM

There's another thing. If a major objective of public argument is to facilitate rational decision processes within members of an audience, then we have to evaluate the debate as a whole (not just the performance of individual speakers or teams) in order to see how well it is fulfilling that function. As a matter of fact, if we are conducting or participating in a series or set of debates, then we should consciously monitor the effects of the whole program.

Evaluating a whole debate or program means getting some feedback which will show us what's going on. How do we get that feedback?

For openers, we have available certain unobtrusive measures of the impact of a debate. For instance, do the persons who attend get enough out of it to come back for the next debate you schedule? Do people come in and inquire when the next debate is going to be? For that matter, do they stay through the first one? Although listeners are rather polite, they do find excuses for leaving at an early opportunity any event which is too painful. If they stick around, and if they come back the next time, you are off to a good start. Such matters are not too difficult to keep track of, so systematic attendance records should be kept.

How many listeners take an actual part in the debate? Do they ask questions and make speeches voluntarily, thus suggesting their involvement? If given the opportunity, do they vote to continue the debate or to close it early? Then, do they stay around afterwards and keep talking about the subject? We've seen a room full of people remain more than an hour after a debate was over talking and arguing animatedly among themselves. We took that to be a good sign of the involvement level of that audience.

Naturally, mere attendance and involvement do not automatically mean that you are encouraging rational thinking, but without them you aren't having much impact. To go the next step, unobtrusively, you will keep your ears open and evaluate the quality of thinking going on. You can tell whether the participation you observe consists of relatively well-reasoned discourse or, on the other hand, shrieks and fistfights. You can talk with some of the listeners after the debate is over or at other times when you meet them. Occasionally you may benefit from third hand reports (persons who talked with other persons who saw the debate) or from such resultant artifacts as letters to the editor. All of the foregoing constitutes primarily a process of systematically observing the evidence which naturally comes to hand.

You can also get feedback by asking for it. You can give those who are attending a form to fill out asking them to evaluate various aspects of the debate. If you are utilizing a shift-of-opinion or other type of audience ballot, you can allow space for suggestions for improvement or other open-ended responses to the debate which they have heard.

One helpful question to ask on such a form is "Why did you vote the way that you did following this debate?" or "What evidence and reasoning influenced your decision?" By means of a content analysis of the answers to these questions, you can begin to determine the impact of the argumentation and perhaps evaluate the quality of the thinking which you are inspiring. You are bound to get some joking responses in such a survey, but you also obtain important clues as to the intellectual effects of your debates.

If you are an organization sponsoring a series of debates, or if you are a member of a debating society or an argumentation class, you can conduct a thorough evaluation of what you are doing by systematically attempting to answer the following questions:

(1) Are the topics being used of interest and concern to our audiences?

(2) Is the format being utilized one which is conducive to full participation?

(3) Are the speakers sufficiently well informed about the topics they are debating?

(4) Are the speakers skilled in adapting to the particular audience and to the arguments being presented?

(5) Are the debates well managed by the chairpersons and other participants?

As your course or your debate series progresses, it should get better and better, both in terms of the quality of the argumentation being presented and also in its effect upon listeners and their response to it. Judgments on these factors are an important part of making audience debate a viable and useful activity, adding constructively to the "public sphere."

Chapter 13

Planning and Administration

When the reasoning is sharp, the audience responsive, and the topic vital, a public debate is one of the most exhilarating and intellectually stimulating events imaginable. When no one is prepared, however, the topic ill-chosen, the facilities inadequate, or one of the speakers fails to show up, the debate can be a disaster.

No matter what the size or nature of the group staging a public debate, some degree of management and organization is essential, and any continuing program must necessarily maintain standards of quality and responsibility. The quality has to be sufficient to provide worthwhile experiences for those participating, and the reliability needs to be adequate so that events will go on as scheduled. To provide these elements requires a systematic and efficient organization.

Administrators of public debates, who in effect serve as links between a given debate and public opinion generally, face the necessity of managing these debates properly and the responsibility for giving them societal significance.

For instance, they should be aware of their contribution to public "agenda setting," in that their choice of topics or participants will reinforce agenda setting done by the various media or will influence new directions for public exploration and concern.

For another thing, administrators should also think in terms of their contribution to the actual decision-making processes of the society. In picking topics and in publicizing results they may help to move general public deliberation more strongly toward influence on decision-making bodies such as legislatures or other governmental agencies.

As a third concern, administrators may think of themselves as responsible for contributing to the quality of public dialogue generally, so that all talk and deliberation will gain from the reasoned consideration of significant problems and so that more people are taking part in the deliberation of public affairs.

With such concerns in the back of your mind, when you are involved in administration of public debates you can count on being swamped with pragmatic demands and petty details. Posters won't get printed on time and microphones won't work. While our assumption here will be that we are dealing with a relatively continuous program originating within an educational institution, most of the administrative concerns we'll talk about will face any sponsor of public debates. Whether a program consists of a single debate or an extensive schedule under the direction of a professional forensics staff, you still have to consider such matters as arrangement-making, personnel, publicity, and even budgeting.

GIVING PUBLIC DEBATE A HOME BASE

Public debates don't grow on trees. The best way to make sure that you'll have opportunities to debate is to institutionalize the process in some way. Either set up new organizations or use existing ones to provide continuity and regularity. Some of the organizational possibilities have already been mentioned in Chapter 2, so now we'll simply take a look at what we have to think about in giving debate a "home" of sorts. Even if you are now enrolled in a course where debate takes place pretty regularly, you may want to think about creating another base for participation.

A Debating Society. The notion of a debating society has kind of an old fashioned ring to it, but we all know how to form clubs, so we shouldn't have any trouble modernizing the idea.

A debating society is an essentially self-contained organization which gives its members a chance to talk about important public problems in a debate format at regularly scheduled meetings.

The central operating unit in a debating society will normally be a program committee or its equivalent. What are the debates going to be about? Who's going to be in them? The debates themselves are the central activity of a debating society, and somebody has to figure these things out. Somebody has to be responsible for them. An efficient program committee, responsive to the needs and desires of the membership and alert to emerging public concerns, will assure that meetings are profitable and enjoyable for the members. If the program committee operates only marginally well (or not at all), the whole society suffers. Get good people on your program committee.

The programs aren't usually limited to formal debates, though. The society can from time to time listen to invited speakers, have contest activities, sponsor outside events, and engage in their own social activities. You can have a marshmallow roast.

Next to the program committee, a publicity committee is for some debating societies the busiest group. Especially if debates are to be open to the general public, information will have to be circulated to tell people what's going on. Furthermore, publicity serves to attract membership. And publicity also may well give the views of the members more impact by circulating the results (and even the topics) of the debate through various media.

Depending on the aims of the society, you will have a constitution and the normal collection of officers. One club had separate vice presidents for program, personnel, and publicity, to make sure those jobs got done. Sometimes you'll have appointed officials such as a parliamentarian or sergeant-at-arms.

A Debate Team. The aim of a debate team, usually sponsored by an educational institution, is primarily to engage in debates with teams from other schools. If such contests are conducted as public debates, they may be held at either institution or in other localities, following the principles we have discussed throughout this book.

The debate team is made up of a group of selected individuals who practice, train, and compete under the supervision of a coach or director.

Thus a debate team should normally have fairly strong leadership and support from their institution. A professionally trained and oriented director is highly desirable. In a large debate program, which may include tournament debating and other forensics activities, one faculty member or graduate student should be assigned to manage the audience debate squad.

A Series. Wherever expectations may be established, public debating is more likely to endure. Therefore, if any organization sets out to sponsor a debate, they will develop a better following if they can promise to have regular programs. One answer is the sponsorship of a debate series, where each individual event may be used to reinforce and support the others. If you have in mind putting on a debate, think about making it a series.

Expectations may be developed in other ways, as well. The genre of political debating has become popular enough so that there is frequently a call for debates even though no one is specifically charged with setting them up.

Through debating societies, debate teams, and debates in series, institutional support may develop which will augment the available opportunities for public debate to take place.

ARRANGEMENTS

Whether or not you have "institutionalized" the debate process, there are always plenty of detailed arrangements you have to make in order for the event to proceed smoothly. When you have a regularly meeting argumentation class or debating society, provisions for time, place, and the like become fairly routine most of the time. However, whenever you are setting up a debate, you may well want to have a detailed checklist to follow to make sure everything gets done. We'll mention seven items which should normally be part of any such checklist.

1. For instance, you have to set a time and place. Even on-campus locations are frequently available only when scheduled some time in advance. In a community you have to scout out an appropriate hall and find out who's in charge and whether it will be available. The

scheduled time should be coordinated not only with the participants but with other events which may be going on in the vicinity.

2. The necessary furnishings should be put in place. Chairs, tables and lecterns on the platform, water pitchers, and other equipment when needed, such as chalkboards or easels, should be provided. Sometimes you'll be expected to arrange for janitorial service for the occasion, as well.

3. Special provisions may have to be made for electronic equipment. If the situation requires a public address system, for example, microphones may be necessary not only at the speaker's stand at the front of the auditorium, but also at the tables where the main speakers are sitting and at one or more points in the audience for speeches from the floor. Appropriate equipment (and manpower) must be in place if the debate is to be recorded or broadcast. Life really gets complicated if you are planning to videotape or televise the event.

4. Duplicated programs are a desirable feature for a public debate, indicating not only the participants and the exact wording of the topic, but also the ground rules for audience participation. These must be printed and distributed. Two sample programs appeared as an appendix to Chapter 3.

5. Social amenities may well be on your checklist. Special guests should be welcomed, and even formal receptions may be planned. If you're going to have refreshments, they have to be planned and ordered. Somebody has to pour the punch.

6. The participation of all of the personnel who will be involved in the event should be confirmed. We'll talk more about that in a succeeding section.

7. A final checklist item which will be explained more fully in this chapter is the adequate publicizing of the debate.

When an interscholastic public debate is contemplated, the negotiations become notoriously complex. We suggest using the telephone (or direct conferences when they are feasible) and written confirmation of agreements as well. Normally, one school will issue an invitation to another. The invitation should contain some options wherever possible so that the responding institution will have some fair choices and to make agreement more likely. For instance, several topics may be suggested out of which the responding school may select one which it is prepared to debate. One common procedure is for one team to select the topic and the other to have the choice of sides. Optional dates are desirable in an invitation as well. Formats should be explicitly described. The responding school replies as soon as possible indicating which options it selects, and the school issuing the invitation provides final confirmation of the agreement. Not infrequently further negotiations are necessary before the debate is finally scheduled. A similar procedure may be used by a touring team which desires to debate on various campuses.

Outside of the academic setting, the arrangements for debates may be equally complex. We have earlier referred to the arduous negotiations which take place in setting up a nationally televised debate between Presidential candidates.

The arrangements that are made should be designed to facilitate a meaningful and profitable public debate.

PERSONNEL

One of the advantages of an audience debate is that anybody can be in it. Principal speakers may be invited to participate because of some special expertise with respect to a particular question and their commitments may be limited to a single debate. Other speakers may commit themselves to a whole program and be willing to prepare for a number of topics and for other roles, such as chairpersons, in various debates.

Recruiting, then, for participants in public debates is a necessary but flexible endeavor. In an educational institution, most of the standard methods of recruitment used for any organization, from the tennis team to Le Cercle Francais, may be employed, including organizational publicity, open meetings for interested persons, word-of-mouth publicity, and personal conferences with promising individuals. When public debating is an adjunct of a fully developed forensics program, personnel for audience debates quite naturally emerge from among students engaged in tournament debate, in extemporaneous and persuasive speaking, the speakers bureau, and other activities.

An important feature of public debate as a student activity is that the amount of participation may range from the most minimal, such as mere attendance or perhaps asking a question from the audience at a public forum, up to the acceptance of numerous assignments as a key speaker for a series of debates. Thus it is possible for students to "work up" to increasing amounts of participation if they are so inclined and for administrators to encourage active audience members to accept more formal and extensive roles. Sometimes "a star is born," when an audience member makes such a notable speech that he or she is invited to be a main speaker the next time out.

Generally a stable group or organization, such as a debating society or a debate "squad" as described earlier, will constitute a more dependable pool of prepared participants. The formation of such a society is an appropriate early step in the development of a program of any breadth. Within an organization, the officers, committees, and directors responsible for special functions may carry out a coordinated program of activities. Certain individuals may be delegated to make arrangements, others to prepare, publicize and participate in them. Furthermore, a stable membership permits a necessary accountability and discipline to be maintained. Dependable members are rewarded with more substantial responsibilities with appropriate amounts of honor and glory; goof-offs are discovered and either transformed or, when necessary, disciplined. Finally, the reserve personnel available in the group mean that reserves are available to provide flexibility whenever circumstances such as personal emergencies or illness make someone unavailable for a particular occasion.

The selection of personnel for the major roles of principal, or "constructive," speakers may be handled in a number of ways. For instance, a system of tryouts open to all may be established, with set rules, where those who demonstrate superior qualifications are selected for the job. In some cases, the individuals who are to serve this function are simply chosen by the debate director on the basis of their interests, qualifications and past performance. They may even to some extent simply take turns. Also, because of the close relationship among speakers, topics, audiences and situations in public debate, the selection of key speakers may be made by the committee or individuals who are responsible for planning any given debate.

PUBLICITY

After all, the debating we have been talking about is inherently "public," so publicity is a natural and important part of the enterprise. This publicity should not be left haphazardly to chance, but rather it should be reasonably systematic with someone responsible in charge of it.

Debate publicity has two main functions: (1) specifically to get some people to attend particular debates and (2) more generally to tell as many people as possible what you are doing.

Attendance.   Surprisingly enough, direct publicity for an individual debate is frequently more informational than motivational. The main idea is to make known the time and place of the event, what it's about, who's in it, and the like. Anyone who might be inclined to come and participate needs to know these things. Thus the factual information will generally be the most important feature of any display advertising you do, posters you put up, and notices you send by direct mail. Many newspapers and community oriented radio stations have "calendars" of events in which their readers and listeners can take part, so make sure you get listed there, too. And regular "news releases" are likewise a basic part of any systematic publicity effort.

Beyond such advertising, other channels of communication are frequently available. If, for instance, a debate has one or more sponsoring organizations, appropriate information will normally be distributed to their members. And word of mouth publicity can also be especially effective when it is generated through individuals who are intellectually or socially influential.

We don't have to neglect motivation entirely, though. Even the selection of a topic for debate may be guided to some extent by the interests of potential participants. A "hot" topic may draw a crowd. Appeals in advertising and other publicity may be directed toward individuals or groups with special interests or values, so bankers may be attracted to debates on financial matters and the garden clubs by environmental questions. The mixture of motives which attract audiences, even to "required attendance" in some cases, is reflected in the earlier discussion of the "public" in Chapter 2.

General Publicity. One aspect of general organizational publicity is letting the world know that your organization exists. There is a Debating Society in our community, the League of Women Voters is equipped to sponsor political debates, or the Zoning Commission has regular hearings on the first and third Mondays. A Publicity Committee should have as an explicit objective getting the name of the organization or the debate series, as well as some idea of what kind of activity is involved, into the public consciousness.

A second and more fundamental aspect of general publicity is to extend the impact of the debate and thus further contribute to the public dialog. If debates can be "covered" so that stories in the news media incorporate some of the lines of argument and evidence presented in a debate, then those ideas themselves are given greater circulation. Participants in these events may be encouraged to make themselves available for interviews and talk shows in electronic and print media. Even transcripts of the debates you sponsor may be produced and circulated. When the substance of the debates has substantial news value, the activity increases its impact and its value for public opinion formation and decision making.

BUDGET

Although public debating has a great deal of flexibility in finances as well as in other elements, some of the arrangements we have described do cost money.

Among the items which any sponsoring organization will have to consider paying for will be (1) transportation and housing, (2) meals and other food, (3) hospitality, (4) rental of equipment and facilities, (5) printing of posters and programs, and (6) supplies. Sometimes personal stipends will be necessary to attract professional speakers or visiting teams from other countries. An extensive public debating program should develop an estimated budget for the whole year, and anyone at all conducting even a single debate should work out a budget as part of the planning procedure they employ.

Where will the money come from? In educational institutions, many debate programs are provided with a regular budget from departmental or administrative funds. Occasionally such a budget will be under the auspices of student government or student affairs offices, or they may be partially provided by an endowment or alumni funds. In other organizations, financial needs are usually met through membership dues and special fund-raising efforts.

Some opportunities for meeting expenses are more directly related to specific debates and special occasions. There is a strong "public service" dimension to most audience debating, and groups who respond to an invitation to sponsor or co-sponsor an event will usually help with publicity, facilities, entertainment and other costs. Service clubs and other community organizations who invite you to debate for them can be asked to provide meals and travel expenses. If a debate is part of a school convocation series, the series budget will give some assistance. With appropriate caution, some initiative in contacting special interest groups may lead to money for particular debates or for a debate series.

Charging admission for public debates is apparently an idea whose time has not yet come.

TRAINING

And how do you get better at audience debating? Although, as has been noted earlier, many debaters in schools will have taken advantage of learning opportunities through tournament participation, individual events competition and speakers bureau activities, as well as classes in speech communication, an organized audience debating program will include provision for additional theory and practice which are desirable for prospective participants.

Theory. Members of a debate class or debating society, as well as all individuals who find themselves much engaged in public debate, ought to try to know what they are doing. They are better off if they understand how information is processed and judgments arrived at through argumentation and the debating process. The debates themselves become more productive if principles of constructing, challenging and evaluating lines of reasoning are widely known and when alternatives are recognized.

Naturally, one way to learn theory is to read about it, and of course this book should be required reading for every citizen of the United States of America. Some other books are good, too. One upon which we have relied heavily is *The New Rhetoric*, by C. Perelman and L. Olbrechts-Tyteca. Even traditional textbooks in argumentation and debate, frequently constructed upon foundational premises far different from those we think appropriate for public debating, will give a thoughtful speaker a good deal of wisdom about what may be required in a debate. Journal articles in *Argumentation and Advocacy* can bring people up to date on recent advances in argumentation theory.

Beyond reading about debate theory, groups may also educate themselves through lectures, discussion, and reflective observation of debate in its many forms in our society. You can watch or go to a debate together and talk about it afterwards.

Practice. As we said in the first chapter, there is no such thing as a "practice debate" under the assumptions we are making in this book. All communication is influential. Still, any learning process involves a certain amount of trial and error, so provision for trying out ideas and techniques under conditions where "damage control" is possible has to be part of a systematic training program.

Workshops and exercises give good opportunities for practice. To try out debating techniques and theories, you can institute workshops on, for instance, almost any topic covered in our earlier chapters:

> Research methods
> Finding issues
> Evaluating evidence
> Using warrants
> Asking and answering questions
> Refutation
> Delivery
> Analyzing audiences

In this way members may be able to strengthen all aspects of their personal debating abilities.

Within a workshop atmosphere, substantive arguments on specific topics can be set forth provisionally to "see what happens." In effect, lines of reasoning and sets of evidence may be "tried out" in a controlled context with a limited listenership of others who are engaged in the same process. "Off-the-wall" thinking, even playful or patently insincere talk, may be tolerated and even encouraged for exploratory purposes in such a setting. To "see what happens" means posing ideas where the workshop or class "audience" is most alert to the fact that something a little different is going on.

Thus a workshop environment, or closed sessions of a debating society or academic class, may be as close to a "practice" session as you're going to get. Generally, the learning and training anybody gets will take place in the crucible of general public opinion and reaction.

QUALITY CONTROL

It is time now to go back to the starting point of this book and remember what public debating is all about. It operates, as we said in Chapter 1, in a world of genuine conviction and genuine communication. It is supposed to be rational. And it functions as a constructive force in the public deliberation of actions and values in our democratic society.

All of this means that we're taking part in an eminently significant activity and that quality control is essential. We want to have the best possible public debate. In administering these events, as in participating in them, the pursuit of excellence is vital. The goals of full democratic participation and effective democratic decision-making are central to the whole process.

There are four points we should be especially sensitive about in maintaining quality control in our debates.

1. Keep the public dimension in mind. An audience debate operates in the context of public discourse generally and has value insofar as it contributes meaningfully to it. In choosing topics, in publicity and outreach, and in direct individual involvement, quality is judged by what it all means to the public. We can watch out for the temptation to be merely entertaining or to become a coterie activity with no impact on anything at all.

2. Thorough preparation is imperative. A frequent complaint

about public debating is that it is too superficial and empty
Fortunately, individuals tend to be attracted to debates where they
have personal knowledge and special concerns, but for everyone
there is no substitute for knowing what you are talking about. An
informed citizenry is one goal of public debate and thus a high
quality of research and preparation is a basic standard to be observed.

3. Communicative interaction should be maintained. Formal rules
of procedure as well as the social norms of participation may be used
to ensure intelligent give and take. High standards of quality in
propositional analysis, challenge, response and communication
among all participants are fundamental to the public debate process.

4. Basic ethical standards are vital. Integrity is a difficult factor to
monitor overtly, but good debate will subscribe strongly to such
ethical values as honesty and fairness. The competitive nature of
debate sometimes tempts one to take shortcuts, to try to distort and
confuse rather than enlighten. Therefore, a sensitivity to ethical
perils and a reinforcement of ethical strengths are also vital
components of quality control.

So how do we provide quality control in public debate?
Fortunately, there are some inherent characteristics of debate which
are helpful. The basic format ensures challenge to dubious ideas for
instance. Furthermore, the debates are manifestly public and no one
really wants to look stupid. The audience having ultimate control of
conclusions and decisions means that they can also recognize and
discount irrational or unethical behavior.

Going beyond these inherent constraints, we may also formalize
to some extent the procedures we use to control quality. We may
invite critics to observe debates and provide us with informed
feedback about our content and procedures. We may use forms and
other instruments to evaluate a whole program, as suggested in
Chapter 12. And we may make regular and systematic review of
debate quality, as in special meetings devoted to the subject or post-
debate discussions, a standard practice for our organization. Heavy
disciplinary measures are seldom necessary, but some clubs elect a
sergeant-at-arms just in case. In general it is most useful (and highly
appropriate) simply to talk about good quality in order to be aware of
it and to implement it.

The management of any productive public forum depends upon an attention to detail and efficient planning as well as personnel who are committed to the conduct of really excellent public argument as a contribution to meaningful decision making and a fully functioning democratic society.

Appendix: Resources and References

Note: The items in the following annotated bibliography are intended to give you a glimpse of the possibilities for extending your understanding of public debating. Some of them may seem rather old to the uninitiated and some of them are not easily accessible, but all of them are relevant. *Public Argument* does not pretend to tell you all you need to know about the subject. You are encouraged to read widely about argumentation as well as to practice audience debating as often and as well as you can.

Beatty, Michael J., and Michael W. Kruger ((1978). The Effects of Heckling on Speaker Credibility and Attitude Change. *Communication Quarterly*, 26: 46-50.

This experimental study says that heckling is not a mere distraction. If audience members identify themselves with the heckler, their attitudes toward the speaker and what he or she is saying are significantly more negative than when there isn't any heckling. On the other hand, if they see the heckler as an "outsider," then they'll like the speaker better and agree more strongly with the position being advocated.

Cox, E. Sam, and Scott L. Jensen (1989). Redeeming Part of Debate's Education Mission via Public Formats. *Spheres of Argument: Proceedings of the Sixth SCA/AFA Conference on Argumentation*. Ed. Bruce Gronbeck. Annandale, VA: Speech Communication Assn., 440-445.

This article provides helpful descriptions of specific instances in which debates were conducted by college students for a variety of audiences, along with a lucid explanation of the value of public debates to the participants. The proceedings of this conference, by the way, also include a number of other valuable essays on public debate and the public sphere generally.

DeLancey, Charles, and Halford Ryan (1990). Intercollegiate, Audience-Style Debating: Quo Vadis. *Argumentation and Advocacy*, 27, 48-57.

DeLancey and Ryan present in a nutshell the salient features of intercollegiate audience debating. They provide a rationale for rhetorical and programmatic values of this activity as well as helpful and realistic descriptions of the administrative demands of setting up such debates. Their article describes well the ways in which a competitive debate program may feature public argument.

Ehninger, Douglas, and Wayne Brockriede (1978). *Decision by Debate* (2nd ed.). New York: Harper and Row.

This important text was the first to make explicit applications of the Toulmin model of the warranting process. The authors stress that argument is context dependent and this second edition especially recognized the "person-centered" nature of public argumentation. You can even read Brockriede's explanation of his provocative view of "arguers as lovers."

Fisher, Walter R. (1987). *Human Communication as Narration: Toward a Philosophy of Reason, Value, and Action.* Columbia, SC: University of South Carolina Press.

The observation that "humans are essentially storytellers" is at the heart of the narrative paradigm, here set forth as an alternative which subsumes the rational world paradigm of argument. Since some stories are better than others, since narrative breaks down fact/value dualisms and since all persons have the capacity to be rational in the narrative paradigm, this makes an especially appropriate approach to public debating.

Freeley, Austin J. (1993) *Argumentation and Debate: Critical Thinking for Reasoned Decision Making* (8th ed.) Belmont, CA: Wadsworth Publishing Company.

Freeley's *Argumentation and Debate*, refreshed through frequent revisions, is without doubt the standard textbook in its field. Written from the perspective of educational debate, it is not especially audience-oriented, but it provides you with admirable coverage of the fundamentals of analysis, evidence, reasoning, case-construction and refutation in the debate process.

Goodnight, G. Thomas (1982). The Personal, Technical, and Public Spheres of Argument: A Speculative Inquiry into the Arts of Public Deliberation. *Journal of the American Forensic Association*, 18, 214-227.

In an influential essay, Goodnight delineates some significant aspects of the public sphere while distinguishing it from personal and technical groundings of argument. The latter, he contends, erode the public sphere. This article is one of many that express concern about the decay of the public sphere and take a stab at suggesting remedies.

Habermas, Júrgen (1991). *The Structural Transformation of the Public Sphere: An Inquiry into a Category of Bourgeois Society*. Tr. Thomas Burger. Cambridge, MA: The MIT Press.

The introduction to this book refers to it as "A historical-sociological account of the emergence, transformation, and disintegration of the bourgeois public sphere." By a noted European scholar, it is a challenge to read, but gives you insight into the "bigger picture." A typical segment is on "Institutions of the Public Sphere."

Perelman, Chaim, and L. Olbrechts-Tyteca (1969). *The New Rhetoric: A Treatise on Argumentation.* Tr. John Wilson and Purcell Weaver. Notre Dame, IN: University of Notre Dame Press.

"Argumentation is a function of the audience being addressed," is the bold claim of *The New Rhetoric.* Here we find the richest available lode of fresh audience-centered concepts of rhetoric, including starting points, quasi-logical arguments, and the dissociation of concepts. If you can afford only one book, then read *The New Rhetoric* instead of *Public Argument.*

Rieke, Richard D., and Malcolm O. Sillars. 1989. *Argumentation and the Decision Making Process* (2nd ed.). Glenview, Ill.: Scott, Foresman.

This textbook, designed for Argumentation and Debate courses in Speech Communication Departments explicitly presents "the communicative, audience-centered basis of argumentation." Matters such as analysis, evidence, refutation, and language use are explained largely from an audience-centered perspective. This book also concludes with substantial attention to "specialized fields" of argumentation, such as law and religion.

Toulmin, Stephen E. (1958). *The Uses of Argument.* Cambridge: Cambridge University Press.

Stephen Toulmin released argumentation from the iron grip of formal, demonstrative logic in *The Uses of Argument* and much subsequent writing. Here jurisprudence rather than mathematics becomes the model for the reasoning process. The well-known "Toulmin model" gets its first and fullest explanation in *The Uses of Argument.*

Index